CARAVAN OF
NO DESPAIR

Also by Mirabai Starr

Saint Francis of Assisi: Brother of Creation

Saint Teresa of Avila: The Passionate Mystic

The Showings of Julian of Norwich: A New Translation

God of Love: A Guide to the Heart of Judaism, Christianity and Islam

Mother of God Similar to Fire (with William Hart McNichols)

Saint John of the Cross

Our Lady of Guadalupe

Teresa of Avila: The Book of My Life (translator)

Saint Michael the Archangel

Hildegard of Bingen

The Interior Castle: New Translation and Introduction

Dark Night of the Soul: New Translation and Introduction

CARAVAN OF NO DESPAIR

A Memoir of Loss and Transformation

Mirabai Starr

sounds true
BOULDER, COLORADO

To Ram Dass, lifelong friend and mentor,
and, of course, to Jenny,
who transformed everything.

Come, come, whoever you are!

Wanderer, worshipper, lover of leaving.

It doesn't matter!

Ours is not a caravan of despair.

Come!

Even if you've broken your vow a thousand times,

Come, yet again, come, come.

INSCRIPTION ON RUMI'S SHRINE IN KONYA, TURKEY

(TRANSLATION: COLEMAN BARKS)

Prologue

This was not the way I had pictured this day. The first copy of my first book lay splayed on the kitchen table like a bruise. Dark Night of the Soul, by the sixteenth-century mystic John of the Cross: the quintessential teachings on the transformational power of radical unknowing, of sacred unraveling and holy despair. Its black and purple cover thinly shot with the possibility of dawn. My mother and sister were taking turns thumbing through the pages and making appreciative comments while I paced.

I picked it up, put it back down, and resumed my post at the window.

Thirty minutes after UPS truck had delivered my new book, the police pulled into the driveway. This was not a surprise. My daughter Jenny had been missing since the night before, when she tricked me and took off in my car. All night I rose and fell on waves of turmoil and peace, fearing she would never return, certain that all would be well.

Now our tribe had mobilized. Mom and Amy had cleaned Jenny's messy room so that it would feel good when she came home. Friends had gathered like strands of grass and woven a basket of waiting. Others fanned out in search parties across Taos County, from the Rio Grande Gorge Bridge to the Colorado border.

"Ms. Starr?" An impossibly young state cop stood at the front door, holding a clipboard. A more seasoned trooper stood behind him, hands clasped behind his back. "I'm Officer Rael, and this is Officer Pfeiffer."

"Did you find her?"

Officer Rael took in the halo of heads that gathered around me in the doorway. Friends and family, straining for news. "Would you please step outside, ma'am?"

"Is she in trouble?"

"We need to speak to you in private," said the teenager-in-uniform.

"Okay, but not without my mother."

Officer Rael nodded. I reached for Mom's hand, and we stepped onto the porch.

The policeman got straight to the point. "There's been an accident."

"Is Jenny okay?" I grabbed his arm. He looked down at my hand.

"Your daughter has passed away, Ms. Starr."

Passed away?

"How do you know it's my daughter?" Maybe they had confused her with some other dead girl. "How do you know it's Jenny?"

Officer Rael smiled a little. "The purple hair," he said. "The report you filed described her hair as curly and . . . purple." He cleared his throat. "The victim matches this description."

Victim.

"Where is she?"

"She's been taken to the mortuary." He looked down at his clipboard, as if he had forgotten his next line and had to consult the script. "Ms. Starr, we are going to need you to come and identify the body."

The body.

"How did it happen?" My voice was calm, as though I were inquiring about the final score in a soccer game. "Is anyone else . . . dead?"

"She lost control speeding down the east side of U.S. Hill, almost to the Peñasco turn-off," he said. "She was alone."

Alone—my baby died alone.

My thighs melted and my kneecaps stopped working. I slid to the cement slab and kept going until my arms and legs were outstretched.

"No," I whispered. And then I was wailing. "No!"

In a dark night of the soul (as I had explained in my little book) all the ways you have become accustomed to tasting the sacred dry up and fall away. All concepts of the Holy One evaporate. You are plunged into a darkness so impenetrable that you are convinced it will never lift. You may flail about for something—anything—to prop you up, but you grasp only emptiness. And so, rendered reckless by despair, you let yourself fall backward into the arms of nothing.

This, according to John of the Cross, is a blessing of the highest order.

Tell that to the mother of a dead child.

Part 1

CHAPTER 1

Becoming Mirabai

I had just turned fourteen and was about to become Mirabai. A couple of teachers at Da Nahazli, our "free school" in Taos, came back from their most recent trip to India with a comic book depicting the life of the sixteenth-century Rajasthani princess who gave up everything for Krishna, Lord of Love, and became a wandering God-intoxicated poet and singer. Our eighth-grade class produced a musical play based on the legend of her life. I was cast as Mirabai. I thought it would be perfect if Phillip, my boyfriend, played Krishna, but instead the Lord of Love was being portrayed by a girl named Wendy. It wouldn't have worked out anyway. Phillip had died halfway through rehearsal season, before I had the chance to apologize for refusing to give him my virginity.

I liked Wendy, but I was not in love with her. I was in love with Phillip. Or I used to be. Now I was becoming Mirabai, and I was falling in love with Krishna.

We were getting ready backstage, an adobe room attached to the great geodesic dome at the center of the Lama Foundation, a spiritual community high up in the Sangre de Cristo Mountains. Sarada, our music teacher, wrapped me in her own wedding sari: yards and yards of pale, creamy silk bordered in gold. She brushed my long red hair and placed a jeweled bindi on my third eye. My feet were bare, and tiny silver bells encircled my ankles. There were a dozen yellow bangles riding up each arm, and filigree earrings hung halfway down my neck. My blue eyes were rimmed with kohl.

"It's time," Sarada whispered in my ear, and she gave me a gentle nudge. Surya, our drama teacher and Sarada's husband, pulled the rope to open the heavy wooden door, and I walked through.

The dome was filled with people: parents, siblings, the residents of Lama, and the extended Taos community. But I did not see them. I walked to the altar set up center stage and prostrated myself before the statue of the blue-skinned god playing his bamboo flute, just like we rehearsed. Sandalwood incense was curling up to the vaulted roof. When I lifted my head from the rough pine planks, I noticed a kind of liquid light rising up through my folded knees into my body and infusing every cell. Some dry land inside me sprang to life and burst into bloom. My little girl voice evaporated, and the ecstatic song of a long-dead singer cascaded from my mouth.

"Hare Krishna, Hare Krishna!" I chanted, "Krishna Krishna, Hare Hare!"

Mirabai stepped in, and I was gone. It was a big relief to get out of her way.

A year later, my fake spiritual teacher (who was lurking in the audience that day, watching me blossom) formally bestowed the name of Mirabai upon me in a pseudo-ceremony on a rock in the middle of a river in California. He called Ram Dass, a genuine spiritual teacher, in New York and asked him to sanction my naming. It made sense: I was madly in love with an unavailable god, to whom I composed illustrated poems and sang songs, and I was a tragic figure. Ram Dass agreed.

Who wouldn't want to be named after Mirabai, part superhero and part saint? The legend begins when Mirabai is a small child. She is standing on the balcony with her mother, watching a wedding procession go by. The bride and groom, dressed in exquisite finery, are riding side by side upon the backs of equally bedecked elephants. Beautiful girls scatter marigold blossoms before them, and musicians and dancers follow behind. Everyone seems ecstatic. Little Mirabai is besotted. She points to the man and woman on the elephants.

"Who are they, Ma?" she asks. "What are they doing?"

"They are getting married, little one."

"I want to get married!"

"You already are," her mother says. "Your husband is Lord Krishna."

She takes her daughter by the hand and leads her inside to the family shrine, where brightly colored statues and ornately framed pictures of Krishna adorn the low carved table and wall above it. Mirabai's mother demonstrates how to bow at the feet of the Holy One and offer your heart. With the literal inclinations of a child, Mirabai takes it all in with grave regard. She presses her forehead to the floor and calls out in silence. "Come be my love," she whispers. "And I will never leave you."

And she never does.

But Mirabai's father has other plans for her—namely, to hook up with a prince and elevate the family's status. She is engaged by six and forced to marry by sixteen and move into the palace of her middle-aged husband. As far as Mirabai is concerned, she is already married to Lord Krishna, and she treats her mortal marriage as a charade. She goes through the daily motions of her wifely duties like a sleepwalker. At night she wakes up and sings to her beloved till dawn, entering ecstatic trance states that initially embarrass and ultimately infuriate the prince's household.

They decide to get rid of her.

Mirabai's sister-in-law sends a bouquet of flowers as a peace offering. Nestled inside is a venomous snake. Mirabai inhales the fragrance of her beloved, and the viper slips away. Her mother-in-law offers a cup of exotic fruit juices laced with venom. Mirabai sips the essence of her beloved, and the drink becomes pure nectar. Her father-in-law arranges to have a pallet of rose petals set up in her chamber, secretly covering a bed of toxic nails. When Mirabai lies down to sleep, she embraces her beloved, and the spikes dissolve into flowers.

The prince is less crafty. Heart contorted with jealousy toward an invisible yet infinitely powerful adversary, he draws his sword and charges into Mirabai's chamber, where she is lost in love at the feet of her bronze beloved. But when he sees his wife's face radiant and transported, when he hears the clear-water ripple of her voice as she sings to God, when he enters the sphere of that burning, the locks on the doors of his own heart melt and slide off. He opens. He gets it. He becomes her devotee and offers himself to Krishna. And then he is forced to go off and fight the moguls, where he dies in battle.

Mirabai's in-laws try to get her to commit sati, ritual sacrifice, in which a woman is obliged to throw her own body onto her husband's funeral pyre. But they have the wrong husband. Krishna is not dead. Krishna will never die.

Mirabai manages to escape the palace and flee to Brindaban, where she spends the rest of her life singing, dancing, and composing ecstatic love poems to God. In the end, Krishna reciprocates her devotion when he appears to her on the banks of the Yamuna River and calls her to himself, and they merge into one.

•

Soon after my naming, I followed the lead of my namesake and left home to track the footprints of my beloved. But I got all mixed up and drank the poison. I lay down on the bed of nails and embraced the snake.

CHAPTER 2

Matty

Phillip was not the first dead boy I loved. When I was six and my brother Matty was nine, he was diagnosed with a malignant brain tumor. A year later he was gone. My sister, Amy, had just turned four when Matty died, and Roy was newborn. Mom was in her second trimester with her youngest child when her oldest became sick, and her pregnancy was shrouded in despair. Matty, a baseball fanatic, had named Roy after his favorite player, and Roy has carried his name like a treasure map left to him by his invisible big brother, which never quite led him to the gold of connection.

Matty died on December 28, 1968. Although he was only a child at that time, he had a well-developed political conscience. He plastered the walls of his room with pictures of Martin Luther King Jr., including a photo of Dr. King in his casket from the cover of TIME Magazine. At night he listened to the "I Have a Dream" speech over and over again on his portable phonograph until he could recite the words along with his hero, with all the inflection of a black Baptist preacher. He grew out his sideburns so that he would resemble his other idol, Bobby Kennedy. He wrote to President Johnson and expressed his conviction that the Vietnam War was a big mistake and that the commander in chief should end it immediately. Johnson wrote back thanking the young citizen for his social engagement, and Matty taped the letter to his closet door.

Of course, Matty wasn't politicized in a vacuum. Our parents, liberal Jews, were already active in the antiwar movement. After Matty's death, as the war ramped up, so did our mother's activism. Mom had taught herself to play the guitar so that she could sing protest songs. Now she convened hootenannies at our suburban Long Island home, and folk singers from all over New York gathered in our living room to drink wine, smoke cigarettes, and launch their complaints against the Establishment through music—Bob Dylan, Joan Baez, and Pete Seeger ("We Shall Overcome," "Blowin' in the Wind"), Irish folk songs ("Roddy McCorley," "Danny Boy"), and old American ballads ("She Walks These Hills in a Long Black Veil")—sung in three-part harmony, accompanied by banjo and harmonica. Mom sang us anti-war songs as lullabies every night when she put us to bed ("Last Night I Had the Strangest Dream," "Where Have All the Flowers Gone?" "If I Had a Hammer").

My parents came from opposite sides of the Jewish tracks. My father grew up in an upscale neighborhood in Brooklyn, the son of a wealthy doctor and a socialite who had divorced her first husband (Dad's birth father, a business tycoon) because he bored her. My father had a prep school education and a degree in English literature from New York University. My mother's parents were working-class people from the Bronx. My maternal grandfather always had a longing for country life, so when my mother was small, he moved his family out to Long Island, where he planted honeysuckle hedges and cultivated raspberries. At first my paternal grandparents were not thrilled by their son's choice of a wife, but they came to adore my smart and lively mother as their own daughter.

"She's a firecracker, that one," Grandma would say of our mom. Grandpa, pipe clenched between his teeth, eyes twinkling, would nod in agreement.

Amy, Roy, and I were staying with our grandparents in Brooklyn when Matty lay dying in the children's hospital in Manhattan. It was his third and final hospitalization, at the end of a long year of near deaths and false hopes. Christmas had passed a few days earlier, Hanukkah a week before that. Amy had just turned four on December 20, which also happened to be our father's thirty-ninth birthday.

My parents spent every hour of those final days at Matty's bedside, watching him slip between their fingers like a wave rising, then falling, then surging inexorably back to the sea. It wasn't until two days before the death of their son that Mom and Dad finally surrendered and drove out to the end of the island to choose his gravesite at a historic Jewish cemetery.

After Matty took his last breaths, my father must have called from the hospital to tell his parents it was over, because by the time Mom and Dad walked through the door of the stately brownstone, Grandma and Grandpa had gathered us in their living room. Amy and I sat side by side on the uncomfortable damask love seat, and Roy lay in his bassinette. Mom picked up my little sister and sat down with her in a chair, pressing her face into Amy's soft blond hair. Dad sat down next to me on the sofa and pulled me into his lap.

"Matty died today," he said.

"I know," I said, but I didn't.

I have no idea why I said that, except that I must have wanted to prove that I knew everything and could handle anything. I was a big girl, and now I would be even bigger. I had gone from being the youngest child before my sister was born to the middle child after Amy's birth, and now, in a flash, I'd become the oldest with Matty's death.

But I knew nothing. I didn't know why my grandfather crying made me feel like laughing. I didn't know how I would explain to my third-grade teacher that my brother died over Christmas vacation. I didn't know why I never saw Matty again after the ambulance came to get him that last time.

•

It must have been some time in early November when they took him away. His second remission had come and gone like lightening, and he was sick again, puffed up with cortisone, slow and sluggish. I was used to my slim, athletic big brother and neither recognized nor appreciated this imposter. That Halloween, I raced out the door in my tiger costume, whiskers quivering with glee.

"Come on, slow poke!" I yelled at the limping pirate lagging behind me. I looked both ways and then sped across the cul-de-sac, swinging my plastic pumpkin basket.

Suddenly I heard Mom calling from the doorway, her voice uncharacteristically shrill: "No running!" I stopped in my tracks as if struck by a stun gun. Something was very wrong here.

Soon afterwards, Matty took his last ride to the hospital.

"Can we have the siren on?" he asked our mother, who sat with him in the back, stroking his hair. Mom leaned forward and whispered in the ear of the EMT, who had been trying to keep things quiet so they wouldn't scare their young patient. He tapped the driver on the shoulder, who smiled and flipped the switch. The siren wailed as they careened down the Long Island Expressway.

●

It has taken my mother forty-five years to fill us in on the details of Matty's dying: the day of the diagnosis; my grandfather's consultations with the specialists; the names of each doctor on Matty's team and what their role was in his care; how Mom was in a phone booth talking to the babysitter when she saw one young physician come outside after being with Matty and lean against a wall and weep; how my parents brought in Matty's record player toward the end and played Herb Alpert and the Tiajuana Brass Band—Matty's favorite music—at full volume so it would penetrate his muffled hearing, and a nurse came in and snapped at them to turn it down; how when he could no longer speak they improvised a means of communication so that he could spell out what he wanted through a series of weak squeezes of their hands and what he wanted was Jell-O and this made them very happy.

"It was if there was a jagged precipice around my memory of that time," my mother says. "I couldn't get too close. I couldn't stand it."

For Mom, each telling seems to soften that edge, and she grows bolder. And with every story, a little more of her pain slips into that abyss and is absorbed. It turns out the void is not empty after all. It is filled with love.

When Matty died, I got his stuffed dog, whom I named Cuddles. By the time Matty had received this particular toy in the hospital, he was too sick to play with it, so when I inherited Cuddles, he was nearly new. His fur was tan, he had floppy ears and big brown eyes, and he smelled like grass after a rain shower. Cuddles became my message in a bottle. My personal interpreter of the secret language of death. A window to the Other Side. I had him until I was twenty-eight and adopted my first child, and then adopted a husky puppy to keep her company. The live dog tore apart the stuffed dog, and I could not save him.

CHAPTER 3

Odyssey

For a few years after my brother's death, my parents tried to hold their balance as the world shifted beneath their feet. My dad started and lost several businesses and increased his alcohol consumption in proportion to his fiscal failures. Even as my father folded in on himself, my mother hurled herself into activity. She started a gallery in our basement, representing a series of emerging artists determined to defy accepted conceptions of beauty. I had to admit, they defied mine.

At age thirty-three, Mom decided to go back to school, racing through an associate's degree at the local community college and then enrolling in the newly established Stonybrook campus of the State University of New York, where she studied philosophy, focusing on alternative lifestyles. We began to take family vacations to some of the communes that were proliferating along the Eastern Seaboard, ostensibly to do research for a book my mom was planning to write about communal living. But my parents were getting Ideas.

One of those ideas caught fire on a summer day at the beach and burned down what was left of the landscape of our old life.

We had won a family membership to the Long Island Beach Club in a raffle for our local library. My parents were big supporters of the library. We all had library cards before we had even learned to read, and three years in a row I had won the library-sponsored contest for which elementary school student read the most books over summer vacation. With the money that had been donated to memorialize their son, my parents had commissioned my mother's brilliantly talented art teacher, an alcoholic Holocaust survivor named Vivian, to create an abstract bronze sculpture of the Pieta in front of the Wantagh Public Library.

"Mary was a Jewish mother, too!" Vivian had shouted, always ready for a fight. "And Jesus was a Jewish boy!"

As we sat on the beach that day, taking advantage of our free pass, surrounded by middle-class families with their shiny new beach stuff and appropriate attire, I was struck by how out of place we were.

For one thing, our food was weird. While regular families withdrew bologna sandwiches on Wonder Bread from their Igloo ice chests, we were eating Deaf Smith peanut butter and honey on slabs of homemade whole wheat bread, which we had carried from the car in hand-woven baskets. Other mothers wore one-piece gingham bathing suits with demure skirts. Ours wore a red bandana as a halter-top and a bikini bottom she must have had since high school; it was apparently once was white and now blended in with the clamshells scattered around us. Dad was using an old necktie as a headband around his long black hair, and one leg of his blue-jean shorts was cut longer than the other. While other families reclined on beach chairs with matching umbrellas, we sprawled upon an Indian bedspread.

Amy and Roy could almost pass for ordinary children as they played in the sand, as long as you didn't know that Roy, with his oversized t-shirt, long brown hair, enormous green eyes, and thick black lashes was actually Amy's brother, not her sister. Their beach pail was cracked, and they dug with a wooden spoon instead of a plastic shovel. Every time Amy filled her bucket and turned it over, pressing the molded sand carefully onto the beach at her feet, Roy knocked it down. Amy would groan and Roy would cheer. They seemed to find this game inexplicably entertaining.

I shook my head in contempt and went back to my book: Harriet the Spy. Did I ever get on my big brother's nerves as much as these two annoyed me? I doubted it. I began glossing over all the times Matty stormed into his room and slammed the door to get away from me, recasting us as replicas of Jem and Scout Finch, united against racism and injustice, determined to liberate the enslaved and embrace the Boo Radley's of this world. Until cancer struck down my hero and left me to fend for myself.

It was a perfect East Coast summer day. My parents lay on the beach as if in a trance, lulled by the high sun and low tide. Suddenly my mother sat up, turned to my father, and said, "Let's get out of here."

"Okay." My father shrugged and began to gather up the towels.

"No, I mean New York. Suburbia. This." She swept the crowded beach with her hand, bangles jingling.

"Okay," Dad said again. And a light that had gone out in his eyes sometime between Matty's diagnosis and death began to rise again and spread across his face.

●

By New Year's Day of the following year, 1973, we were gone.

My parents sold the house and, in keeping with their newfound Zen sensibilities, gave away almost everything we owned—heirloom jewelry and silver, an extensive art collection, toys and games, clothing and linens and kitchenware—and dropped off the last of Matty's things at the Salvation Army. They bought a four-door red GMC pickup truck with a cab-over camper and a "Good Sam Club" sticker on the back window, which I desperately wanted to remove because I thought it made us look like Republicans, but which my father insisted would prevent too much scrutiny from the authorities. Apparently my father anticipated some potentially illegal activity.

We piled in and set out on a road trip that would take us from Miami Beach through the Texas heartland, from the Gulf of Mexico to the jungles of the Yucatan, from the counterculture communities of Aspen and Mendocino to the art colony of Taos, where we settled at the foot of the sacred and temperamental Taos Mountain, who welcomed us home and also, like any good goddess, demanded her blood sacrifices.

●

It was late January when we pulled onto the single-track sand road off the highway to Belize and headed toward the coast. We had been traveling for three weeks and were ready to get off the road. In her lap my mother had a hand-sketched map that some fellow vagabonds had made for us at the Mayan Trailer Paradise in Merida.

"You can't tell anyone else about this place," Verna had said, handing her the directions to the secret beach in the state of Quintana Roo, where she and her husband, Rob, had been camping all winter.

"Top secret," Rob agreed. "The others made us swear we wouldn't divulge the location."

"But you guys are an exception," Verna hastened to add. "Now, who wants another scoop?"

We three kids held out our plastic bowls like Oliver.

After running into our family at the swimming pool earlier that day and being invited to smoke a joint with my parents, the Canadian couple had reciprocated by bringing us all over to their campsite for fresh coconut ice cream after dinner, which Verna made in a hand-cranked ice cream maker under the awning outside their RV. We had never tasted anything so beautiful.

The minute we turned onto the tiny jungle lane a few days later, we wondered if we had made a mistake. Our giant camper lumbered along, swaying precariously in the soft sand, enclosed on every side by thick foliage that ripped and fell as we passed. But there was nowhere to turn around, and the Canadians had warned us that it would seem like it took forever to get there and was worth the wait.

We entered a dream. Time melted around the edges, our monkey chatter stilled, and the only sounds were the squeaking of the truck's shocks and the trilling of a dozen varieties of tropical birds. And then, all of a sudden, the jungle broke open onto an expanse of luminous white beach, with the pale turquoise hues of the Caribbean just beyond. My father hit the brakes, jammed the clutch, and we stared in awe. He turned off the ignition, and we sat for a moment in stunned silence, then tumbled out of the truck from all sides like bees released from their hive. We were sighing, squealing, and silent, each according to their temperament.

Roy ran straight for the water, and Amy followed. I ran after them to boss them around and make sure they didn't get eaten by sea monsters, since we seemed to have entered a mythic realm where the inhabitants could not be merely human and the rules were unpredictable.

We lived on that isolated Caribbean Beach on Mexico's Yucatan Peninsula for nearly six months, and we remained in a magical world the entire time. Looking back, I cannot distinguish what happened from what I imagined. Amy and I took long walks on the empty beach that led us into fairylands where driftwood logs turned into goddesses, and when we entered the sea, we became mermaids and swam with our long-lost mermaid sisters. Established quotidian rhythms gave way to a more spontaneous schedule: we slept when we were tired, woke when we were rested, and ate when we were hungry. My parents cooked over a campfire, and we wore little or no clothing. We pooped in a pit nestled in a jungle clearing, over which one of the few hippie travelers that passed through our personal paradise had built a tall toilet open-air seat we called "the throne."

We listened to the same albums over and over on the portable eight-track tape player: the Beatles's Abby Road, the Grateful Dead's Workingman's Dead, Janis Joplin's Pearl, the Moody Blues's Every Good Boy Deserves Favor. Amy and I painted Roy's face with water-colors. I read to them from The Brown Fairy Book and The Purple Fairy Book and The Yellow Fairy Book, which carried us through our entire stay. And I sat alone on the beach for hours at a time, writing poetry in my sketchbook, which I illuminated with Magic Marker borders.

We were almost, but not quite, the only gringos on the beach. Around a hundred yards up from our campsite was a thatched palapa inhabited by a young couple from Georgia. Ramón (well, his name was Ray, but everyone seemed to take on the Spanish version of their name down here) and Willie (easy to pronounce in any language) were both high-powered journalists working for a big-city paper in their old life, but had dropped out by their late twenties. They had already traveled around the world. They were in Turkey and Morocco before they came to Mexico. Whenever the weather was cool, Ramón wore his hand-woven jalaba from North Africa, which made him look like a Bedouin shaman. Willie was a sweetheart, but Ramón was a curmudgeon. Willie made us hushpuppies from the Bisquick she brought back from her last trip home to the States, fried to a golden crisp on the outside and fluffy white within, studded with tiny jewels of chopped onions. She also made banana cream pie with Nilla wafers and instant pudding mix. Food had become our big entertainment.

Ramón didn't speak much, and when he did, it was usually a sarcastic remark. He didn't try to hide how pissed off he was that Rob and Verna had violated the pilgrims' code and drawn a treasure map to his personal Shangri-la. His dislike of children was equally obvious. And four-year-old Roy, who seemed to have internalized all of that in-utero trauma and become an uncontrollable bundle of fury, reinforced Ramón's prejudice every chance he got.

Each member of our family seemed to have a different response to our neighbor's negative attitude. My mom pursed her lips in a kind of flirtatious pout and locked his gaze with hers. Dad turned away and lit another cigarette. Roy tried to smack him. Amy ignored him altogether. And my own eyes would fill with tears as I wondered why he had to be so mean. Mom thought it was because Ramón had polio when he was six and spent much of his childhood in an iron lung, and now one of his legs was thick and muscular and the other dangled from his hip like a rope he dragged along behind him.

I was pretty sure that unless he was criticizing some insipid thing I accidentally said when I was nervous, Ramón did not even notice my existence. But on the morning of my twelfth birthday he surprised me with a gift. It was not wrapped, and it was not new. But it was clearly cherished: a well-worn copy of A Coney Island of the Mind by Lawrence Ferlinghetti. Inside the front cover Ramón had inscribed (in the artless scrawl of a preadolescent boy), "It's possible that sometime you'll be walking along beside a dike. If you have this book, you can roll it up and stick it in the hole and save the multitudes."

I read that collection of poems from beginning to end, and then from the end back to the beginning. Each piece felt like it had been written just for me, even when I didn't understand the nuances of the Beat Generation. The only other birthday present I had received that day was an abalone bracelet from my parents. But after everyone took turns trying to clasp it around my wrist, it became clear that it was not going to fit. It was a child's bracelet, and I was becoming a woman. The single person who seemed to notice this fact was a man I thought didn't even know or care that I was alive. Instead, he recognized me as a serious poet.

Which is what I became. A poet. And very, very serious.

CHAPTER 4

Da Nahazli

Although my parents' parenting skills were disintegrating by the minute, they still placed a high priority on our education. So they chose to settle in the high desert village of Taos, New Mexico, primarily because it was home to Da Nahazli School, where children between the ages of four and fourteen did pretty much whatever the hell they felt like. The philosophy here was that if you allow a child to go where their inner guidance directs them, they will know exactly what they need. Which didn't always work out. My best friend Tot and I, for instance, loved to draw and paint and produce plays and write short stories (actually Tot, at age eleven, was hard at work on a novel), but we weren't guided to balance fractions or memorize the kind of representation afforded by three branches of government.

Our math teacher (who happened to have been sleeping with one of his twelve-year-old students) hypothesized that the reason Tot and I were rebelling against the standard sixth grade mathematics curriculum was because we were too brilliant for mere numerical calculations and cheesy word problems involving cans of soup and pockets of change. So he devised a private tutorial in trigonometry especially for Tot and me. It took around three days before we all surrendered to reality (which in our case meant returning to practicing Serbo-Croatian folk dances with our favorite teacher, Jean). The truth is, Tot probably was capable of grasping the most complex and abstract mathematical concepts—including their philosophical implications—but I could not balance a fraction to save my life, because numbers simply confounded me.

•

Da Nahazli was the hub of the alternative Taos community. We filled the eleven rooms of a crumbling hacienda in the center of town, where distinctions between student and teacher, children and parents, members and visitors were fluid, almost irrelevant. Taos Pueblo elders taught us that the earth is our mother while East Indian yogis modeled the power of silence. Our social studies teacher, Deirdre, brought a Tibetan holy man named Trungpa Rinpoche down from Boulder, Colorado, and he read us Escape From Tibet around the kiva fireplace in the Great Room. Deirdre left us the next year to be with Trungpa full-time and turn into American Buddhist master Pema Chödrön. Ram Dass came through between trips to India where his guru, Neem Karoli Baba, had catapulted to the top of the American Spiritual Seekers Hit Parade because of Be Here Now, the book Ram Dass wrote about him at the nearby Lama Foundation.

Natalie Goldberg, fresh from a master's program at Saint John's College across the Rio Grande Gorge in Santa Fe, was our English teacher and developed "writing practice" among our circle of preteens. Georgia O'Keefe was the judge of a children's art contest, and R. C. Gorman drank with our fathers. Peter Fonda and his sister, Jane, showed up to visit fellow Easy Rider cast member Ellie Walker, grandniece of Isadora Duncan and mother of my other best friend, Michelle. We babysat for the children of Dennis, David, and Duane Hopper during crazed parties at the historic Mabel Dodge Luhan House.

•

One weekend toward the end of my first year at Da Nahazli, a group of us hitchhiked up to a spring equinox gathering at the Magic Tortoise, a commune in the mountains north of Taos. I caught a ride with Hunter, my new boyfriend (we had twirled together in the tire swing on the Da Nahazli playground and decided we would make a good couple) and Phillip, his best friend. Hunter was a drummer and Phillip was a guitar player, and they spent most of each school day jamming in the music room.

An elderly Hispanic couple from the San Luis Valley, just over the Colorado border a few miles from the Magic Tortoise, pulled over in their equally elderly Cadillac and picked us up at the Taos Plaza.

"Ay, mi 'jita," the wife swiveled around to reach for my hand once I had positioned myself between the boys in the back seat. "Does your mama know where you're at?"

Good question. I thought so, but I may have forgotten to mention it. No big deal. My friend Jessie lived at the Tortoise with her family in a round tower house, and I often spent weekends up there, roaming between the communal households with Jessie and her sisters, foraging for food and assisting grown-ups in throwing pots on the wheel and splitting firewood.

I shrugged, the woman said, "tsk," and Phillip rolled his eyes. The husband's face was inscrutable beneath his fedora.

They dropped us off at the bottom of the four-mile dirt road, and we hiked up to the commune through the woods. An onlooker might have wondered what was up with three ragamuffin preadolescents trudging up a mountain. One boy (Phillip) was barefoot, torn blue jeans tied with a woven belt, a shirt he made himself from the remnants of an American flag, black hair down to his hips, carrying his Dobro in a battered guitar case. The other boy (Hunter), sandy curls pressed into an aviator cap, walked in Phillip's shadow. The girl (me) dressed in painter's pants and an oversized alpaca sweater to hide my blossoming curves, long auburn hair, dark blue eyes, a sprinkle of freckles across my Jewish nose. I had a leather pouch with beaded fringe tied to my belt loop where I kept a chunk of polished agate gifted to me by my father's closest friend, a self-proclaimed shaman named Jim, a package of Zig-Zag rolling papers and a pinch of pot (mostly for show), a pencil stub and the folded-up poem I was working on, and a vial of jasmine oil.

When we arrived at the Tortoise, the boys disappeared among the throng of kids shooting baskets on the pounded dirt behind Miles's house, and I wandered over to the dwelling of an artist named Annie to find my own friends. I wasn't feeling much like anyone's girlfriend and was trying to decide whether that was good news or bad. Inside, women were laying out pots of black beans and brown rice, bowls of salad, baskets of blue corn muffins, and plates of goat cheese. Three guys sat on the floor strumming a dulcimer, a mandolin, and a tanpura. A couple was making out on the tattered couch.

Jessie rushed down the ladder from the loft, followed by Michelle, who had made her way up the mountain earlier that day and was now squealing my name. "Thank God you're here!" And they threw their arms around me. This was already way better than a boyfriend who had yet to even hold my hand.

Parched from our hike up the mountain, I went over to the food table and poured myself a mug of hand-squeezed lemonade, sweetened with raw maple syrup and infused with fresh spearmint from Annie's garden, and gulped it down. Annie waved at me through the recycled French doors to the back porch, where she was dancing with her toddler, Georgia, to the medieval madrigals wafting from the living room.

"Let's play jacks," Jessie suggested, and we sat down on the kitchen floor. Like a professional gambler, Michelle pulled a little Guatemalan woven zipper bag from the pocket of her sweatshirt and shook out the jacks, grabbing the little rubber ball before it rolled under the stove. We were champions. We had long ago graduated from the basic Onesies to Triple Flying Dutchmen and Threading the Needle. My little sister, Amy, and her best friend, Zoe (Phillip's sister), had become our disciples, and because they practiced so much, they were threatening to outplay us, which was not okay with me. I relished this opportunity to polish my game.

By the time we had finished our first round, I was starting to feel peculiar. The bright yellow ball would fly into the air and not come down for a very long time. A trail of starburst flowed behind it as it landed, bounced, and once again arced slowly into the sky, which had managed to open up beyond the beams of the kitchen ceiling. When I reached to scoop up my pile of jacks, they became tiny bones in my hand, with bits of bloody cartilage still attached. I yanked back my fist and gasped.

"What happened?" Jessie asked.

I shook my head hard, trying to snap back to the familiar world. But I could not clear my head. My friend's voice sounded like it was coming from a long way away, as if she were calling to me from a deep hole in the ground. I turned to look at Jessie's face. Her long lashes fluttered; her teeth gleamed.

Michelle caught the ball as it dripped from my other hand, cocked her head at me, and then exchanged a look with Jessie. Weirdo, the look said.

I couldn't argue with that. I did not feel like myself at all, and the world looked nothing like the one I thought I lived in. I glanced around the room, trying to orient myself with familiar objects: a bottle of ketchup upside down on the Mexican tiled countertop, a string of rosehips drying above the stove, a man named Rama pulling an apple cobbler from the oven. Nothing worked. I was seeing everything as if through the mesh of a screen. I was trapped on the other side of a door that kept me from everyone and everything I had ever known.

"I can't see," I whispered. "I can't hear." And I leapt up and raced outside to see if the fresh air might bring me back.

The boys were taking a break from shooting hoops and had sat down under a juniper tree to smoke a joint.

"Hey!" Hunter called. "What are you guys doing? Want to get stoned?"

I couldn't answer. My breath was roaring in my ears, and my stomach heaved as if I were in a tiny rowboat lost on a stormy sea. Michelle and Jessie had followed me out and stood with arms folded while I raced up and down the path to the outhouse, hoping to outrun the nightmare that was crashing into my waking life. They all stared at me, quiet, confused. The look on their faces terrified me.

"I have to go," I said, my own voice unfamiliar and thunderous. I glanced around, panicking.

Where could I go, and how would I get there?

"You sick?" Hunter asked.

"Yeah. I think so."

"You can lie down in my bed," Jessie offered. I nodded.

My four companions enfolded me like a human blanket, and we

oozed across the clearing to Jessie's house. They guided me up the narrow wooden staircase to the open loft Jessie shared with her mother, father, and baby sister. I lay down on Jessie's narrow foam mattress on the floor beneath the skylight, and Michelle tried to cover me with Jessie's patchwork quilt. I threw it off as if it were a noose. I thrashed, I whimpered, I stared at the ceiling, suddenly transfixed by the network of cobwebs that laced the edges of the deep blue sky, my gaze dripping down to the smooth mud walls, shot through with shards of mica and slivers of straw.

"You want me to stay with you?" Michelle asked. Stay with you stay with you stay with you, a voice echoed behind hers.

"No, thank you," I managed. Thank you thank you thank you. Michelle looked relieved.

One by one, my friends squeezed my hand and disappeared down the steps and away from me. At the top of the stairs, Hunter turned and said, "I'll come back and check on you, okay?" But I could not answer. Some secret hand had reached down through the sky and pulled me up into a shapeless embrace. I had no choice but to surrender. I let go and left this world far behind.

●

At some point Hunter did come back, as he promised, but I could not speak, and pretty soon he drifted away again.

Finally Phillip appeared at the foot of the bed and crouched down beside me. "My dad came to pick us up," he said, searching my eyes. I tried with all my might to focus on his face, his lips, the sound of his voice. He almost seemed to know what I was going through. How could he? "Want a ride home?" Phillip asked.

I nodded and sat up. The sound of an electric guitar and a burst of song drifted over the tops of the piñon trees from across the compound. The music was a magic carpet, come to fetch me. I debated climbing on and taking off, decided against it, and forced myself to concentrate on the task at hand: getting home.

I watched myself follow Phillip down the stairs and out the door into the brilliant blue and gold of the late afternoon. A short Jewish guy from New York, who looked like my father disguised as a normal person, was standing next to a fancy rental car, scrutinizing me as I appeared, blinking and quivering.

"Where do you live, Honey?" Phillip's dad spoke fast. I could not make sense of the question.

"I don't know," I muttered.

"What?"

"I can't remember."

"You don't know where you live? Jesus Christ."

"In the Valdez Valley," Phillip covered for me. "She's sick, Dad."

"Okay, let's get going." He patted me on my faraway head and opened the back door. I slid in beside Phillip. Phillip's dad was visiting his kids from somewhere back east, where he made TV commercials for a living.

The luminous swirls and yawning thrums of the past few hours were beginning to give way to a kind of shadowy quiet that held me in its grip. I could not move—or speak. I could barely breathe, nor did I feel the need for breath. I sat in the backseat and watched the sun fade from the sky and the lights of Taos wink on as we neared the four-way intersection and turned in the direction of the valley where I thought I lived. I hoped the way would reveal itself as we drew closer, but the landscape still made no sense, and the gathering darkness swallowed any vestiges of familiar navigational markers.

"Now what?" Phillip's father barked from the front seat.

I gazed at Phillip's profile beside me, pleading with my eyes, which he could not see. He reached for my hand and stroked it.

"Turn toward the Ski Valley, and then go left instead of right. Their house is near the bottom of the road."

Phillip had only been over to our place once or twice, but somehow he remembered the way and led his father up the deeply rutted driveway. I pretended to be asleep, the only cover I could come up with to justify my utter inability to find my way home.

Mom stepped out onto the porch when we pulled up, and she waved cheerfully. "Did you have a good day?" she asked, as I climbed out of the back seat and staggered toward the house. I shook my head no and rushed inside, straight for my room: a high bed built of pine planks above the water heater in the utility closet. I pushed aside the blanket that served as a door and climbed the ladder to my very own nest, crawling under the covers and straining to feel normal.

It was a long time till I felt anything like normal. Days of dreamlike hours melted into otherworldly weeks, during which I continued to feel as if I were trapped on the other side of a wall, watching the rest of the world through a chink in the stones. Everyone (including radically altered me) was carrying on as if everything was the same as always. It was not the same. It never would be.

On the third day I came home from school, threw myself down at the kitchen table, and began to sob.

My mother came over and sat beside me. She lifted my chin and looked into my eyes. "What is it, my love?"

"I don't know. I think I'm going crazy."

"You have always been sensitive," she said, peeling away a lock of tear-drenched hair from my face, fingering the soft fuzz underneath. "God, your hair is like spun copper!" She loved to say that, parting the dark red outer strands to reveal the pale hair underneath.

"Mom, something's wrong with me."

"Nothing is wrong, my love. You're just turning into a teenager."

Oh my God, was this what becoming a teenager meant? Why didn't anyone warn me? In that moment, I was fairly certain I wouldn't make it. No one could be expected to live through this. For the first time (but not the last) I contemplated how I might end my life and escape.

●

Over the years I would slip in and out of this altered state. Nothing in particular seemed to trigger it. I might be practicing scales on my flute, or stirring a pot of spaghetti sauce, or opening the door to greet a friend who had stopped by for a visit, and suddenly I would feel as if I were dreaming, and I couldn't tell what was real and what was the dream. Or I would be in the middle of a philosophy lecture in graduate school, where I had a teaching fellowship, and as I was drawing a distinction between rationalism and empiricism in epistemology, my words would begin to slide from my tongue and dissolve in the air like soap bubbles. I would have to stop talking, my heart hammering in my chest.

In my mid-twenties I was living on the edge of an old-growth redwood forest in Northern California. One morning, a few friends suggested that we take LSD and spend the day exploring the deep green woods. I had always been terrified of psychedelics. I had worked for years to wrestle my "episodes" under control and thought the drugs might trigger a fresh cascade of altered states.

I decided the fear had loomed like a beast on the outskirts of my life and paralyzed me long enough, and it was time to face it off. I dropped the acid and spent the day frolicking among the giant ferns and moss covered logs of the fairy forest, feeling like a woodland nymph, fascinated by the way the drops of dew clung to the face of a trillium blossom and the branches of the grandmother madrones wove a net of belonging for a hundred kinds of creatures.

At some point, as I leapt across a stream and dove into the hollow of a redwood tree, it occurred to me that this was not an unfamiliar experience. I had first noticed this explosion of color and sound that day at the commune in the mountains when I was twelve. My knees buckled and I gasped: I had accidentally ingested LSD that day. Or mescaline. Or some other radically mind-altering substance that must have been floating around the party. I hadn't lost my mind. I had only lost my innocence. Only I was too innocent to know it.

•

A few years ago I was reminiscing with Annie about the old hippie days in Taos. We were reflecting on both the magic and the recklessness with which parents went about raising kids at that time, and I brought up my experience of having acid slipped to me at a party up at the Magic Tortoise.

Annie's deeply lined face turned pale. She reached for my hand. "It was me," she said.

"What was you?"

"I gave you that acid. It was in the punch. I thought everyone should trip. I wanted to turn on the whole world."

"Even children?"

"I thought it would be a good start."

I didn't know whether to leap from my seat and shake Annie by her frail, velvety shoulders or laugh the whole thing off—all those years of terrifying dissociative states that had catapulted me onto a spiritual path and into the clutches of opportunistic teachers.

I took a deep breath. "I understand," I said. "My father felt the same way, only his target was the government. He thought that if all the most powerful men in the world were to trip on acid at least once, there would be peace on earth."

Annie nodded solemnly. "Yes," she said. "We were trying to make peace."

•

Not long after that spring equinox party, a group of kids, including Hunter and Phillip, were playing Sardines in our haunted house in Valdez during summer vacation.

Sardines is the reverse of hide and seek. One person hides, and then each of the other players searches for that person. When they find them, they quietly slip into the hiding place with them, until all they players are squished in together. The end.

It was my turn to hide. Phillip found me first. I was under the bed in Amy and Roy's abandoned room. He crawled in beside me and wrapped his arm around my shoulder, pulling me close in the darkness.

He began to stroke my back.

I turned my face toward his.

He pressed his nose against mine.

His tongue flicked between his teeth and over my lips.

I gasped, drew back.

He rubbed my back, a little lower.

I kissed him.

And then we were melting into each other, kissing, rubbing our cramped bodies together, my new breasts pressing into his chest, his groin swelling against my belly.

Oh, I said to myself. So this is what a boyfriend is. Hunter had quietly faded out of my life before we had ever gotten around to touching each other.

Terrified, ravenous, I lay inert as Phillip mashed his mouth into mine and warmed every cell in my body with his breath.

Was this really happening?

This was the boy every girl in school wanted to like them. Phillip was adorable. He played the guitar like Eric Clapton and hung out with the silversmiths in Arroyo Seco. He was aloof and poetic. And now he was kissing me as if I were the most beautiful creature on earth. I tried to ignore his pelvis and focus on his long black hair, his doughy lips, the sandalwood scent of his neck.

When the next kid found us, it was obvious that we were now in a relationship.

The rest of that summer we spent all our time together, and when the new school year started, we couldn't bear to be apart. If Phillip was not at my house, I was at his. Phillip's room was a shed built behind his family's home. It had a huge plate-glass window facing south; posters of Jimi Hendrix and M. C. Escher prints on the plywood walls; his beloved Dobro guitar, amp, and a set of conga drums in the corner; and a purple and green Indian tapestry tacked to the ceiling above his bed. Phillip's mom had concluded that I bore too much responsibility for my younger siblings, so when I was at their place I was forbidden from taking care of anyone, and she insisted on serving me home-baked scones and chamomile tea.

One day Phillip's mother ran into my father at the food co-op and asked him how he was feeling about our relationship.

"Sensational," Dad said, filling his a bag with lentils from the bulk grains bin.

"Aren't you concerned that they're sleeping together? Phillip isn't even shaving yet."

"That's why I'm not worried." Dad gave Nora a wink and continued shopping. He related this conversation to Mom and me with great glee the next day.

For me, "sleeping together" meant just that: climbing into the same bed and going to sleep. But not for Phillip. He may have been newly pubescent, yet he was losing no time in exploring the human condition with all his might, and he was starting to leave me in the dust. Already a child prodigy musician, he was playing in Taos bars with adult bands, camping alone in the mountains, and attending all-night peyote ceremonies in the tepee at New Buffalo. And he was ready for sex.

I wasn't. Phillip was my first real boyfriend—more real than I was ready for.

We had been spending the night at each other's houses for months, cuddling and kissing before falling asleep side by side. This was enough for me; it was perfect. Why did he have to slide his hand up under my t-shirt one night and take my nipple between his fingers? Why did he have to guide my hand into his underpants and press my palm against his soft-hard boy body? Why did he have to make me shove his chest with the palm of my hand and ask him to turn around and sleep with his head at my feet?

Reaching out, Phillip pushed me away. It took a while, but the cords of our first love had been cut and were beginning to unravel. By spring of the following year, we were arguing all the time. Every fight left me mortally wounded, and I staggered around school like Ophelia on her way to the river. But Phillip, who used to be so compassionate, didn't even notice. He began to spend weekends with the twenty-year-old chick who ran the Sunbringer, the thrift store at the end of Bent Street. And then one day Tammy came to school wearing Phillip's favorite Levi jacket, and I knew I had lost him.

Unmoored, adrift, I drew pictures of giant eyes with teardrops dripping from the corners, while Phillip leapt into his life and away from me, like a golden stag, or a supernova.

CHAPTER 5

Mexico Again

Dad picked us up from school one day and informed us that Mom and Ramón had taken a drive to Santa Fe and decided to keep going, all the way to Mexico. They had called my father at Joe's, where he cooked and washed dishes, and asked him to ask me if I'd be interested in meeting them at the border. I said I would.

Mom knew that Phillip and I had just had a huge fight. Phillip and his brother had shot at some dogs that were chasing their chickens. They didn't hit them, but still. I had launched an eloquent diatribe about cruelty to animals, and Phillip had flicked the air between us as if I were a mosquito and walked away. I needed to get out of town.

It's not as if Dad was surprised by Mom's spontaneous road trip with another man. Mom and Ramón had been totally into each other ever since they met on the beach in the Yucatan two years before. Although no one spelled it out, Ramón had even moved from Florida to Taos with his wife, Willie, so he could be closer to my mother. Mom had seemed supremely unsurprised when the pair bounced up the dirt road in their van one day, and Willie deposited Ramón and peeled away. Mom politely asked Carlos, my father's best friend and my mother's current lover, to please gather his things and leave, which Carlos, with a good-natured shrug, did.

Dad had already moved out and settled into a one-room adobe shack on the ridge above our house in the Valdez Valley. There he read cards. Many pilgrims came seeking my father's esoteric guidance. He would seat them at the table (a recycled cable spool), pour himself a jelly jar of Tokay wine, light a Pall Mall and let it burn like incense in the ashtray beside him, and take the seeker's hands in his own for a moment.

"Close your eyes, now," he said. "Let's tune." And they would tune.

Then he would unfurl a cosmic weather report, as revealed by the array of clubs, diamonds, hearts and spades. Dad's love of Bridge had shifted to this ancient system of divination in which modern playing cards have their roots.

Dad had started drinking when he got the news that his not-any-more-wife and her lover were running away to Mexico, and he had been drinking ever since.

●

Amy and Roy clamored into the back of the van with me in the Da Nahazli parking lot. They immediately started searching for Herbie, the field mouse that had taken up residence in our dad's vehicle. Roy pulled a wad of dirty tortilla from his pocket and clicked his tongue in hopes of getting Herbie's attention. At six, Roy was fierce. His enormous green eyes glittered beneath a canopy of dark lashes. Late to talk, Roy communicated by biting whoever crossed him. But when I gathered him into my arms and stroked his hair, he would grow quiet and agreeable.

Roy was a loner. He spent most of his time creating complicated scenarios for his plastic army men, using mounds of dirt and fistfuls of tall grass. It was clear from the way he muttered to himself as he played that Roy's worlds were real, inhabited by good guys and bad guys, and that Roy was the hero of his own journey. In the regular world he was often forgotten, but in Roy Land he sallied forth, sword in hand, breeze through his hair, and everyone made way for the king.

Amy was also royalty. Her long blond hair cascaded down to her hips in glimmering waves. Pale blue eyes, plump lips, ivory skin. From the time she could tie her own shoes, Amy began to change her clothes three and four times a day, depending on which way the wind blew. She might start off as a ballerina before breakfast, and by lunchtime she had transformed into a cowgirl. Then she would dress for dinner in a hand-me-down party dress and platform heels five sizes too big that she had rummaged from the free box in front of Amigos Food Co-op. Amy knew what she liked and was quite clear about what displeased her. Hippies who didn't bathe, for instance. Our parents' refusal to have television. Vegetarian food.

At nine, Amy and her best friend, Zoe, were honorary fairies dwelling in Fairyland. They made dolls from hollyhock blossoms, turning the deep red flowers upside down so that the petals became skirts. The little girls enlisted me to help build a pool in the Hondo River below our house using rocks and branches. We called it God's Tear. This is where Amy and Zoe did most of their communing with the Little People.

After Amy finished reading the Narnia books for the second time, she cried. I happened to walk into room just as the sadness was hitting her.

"What's the matter, Ames?"

"I will never be able to go there!" she sobbed. "And I can't stand it."

•

Dad drove us to town with a can of beer between his thighs. We pulled up to the bus depot in Taos just as the sun was setting. It was early March. Winter was still clinging to the valley. I shifted my duffle bag from one shoulder to the other and hugged my father, who swayed a little in my embrace. Then he stepped back and felt around in the pocket of his jeans.

"Here." He slipped a couple of hits of blotter acid (pressed into a book of food stamps) into the bib-pocket of my overalls. "A peace offering for your mom."

"Okay. Bye, Daddy."

"So long, Cookie."

Just like that, I climbed the stairs to the idling bus and found my seat. I gazed out the window as Dad drove away. I watched my town going about its ordinary sunset business as if nothing extraordinary were happening inside this bus, about to grind into gear and head south to the Mexican border.

Mom and Ramón met me in El Paso, and we crossed over the border into Ciudad Juarez, making our way down the west coast to San Blas. We searched for an isolated beach, but those days were over, so we settled for a campsite with reasonable boundaries and set up our tents among the gazillion other campers on Playa de los Cocos. Mom and her lover proceeded to explore their relationship, and I read Justine by Lawrence Durrell, wrote love poems to Phillip in my sketchbook, adopted a flea-infested dog that I took into my tent to sleep with me at night, and walked for miles up and down the beach, seeking solitude. I alternated between determination to do whatever it took to patch things up with the love of my life the minute I got home and breaking up with him once and for all.

Upon my return from one such melancholy sojourn, I found Mom and Ramón sitting on a blanket smoking a joint. This was not unusual. I sat down beside them but did not take a toke. Ever since I had lost my mind at the Magic Tortoise party last spring I had a hair trigger for altered states of consciousness. Someone would say something like, "I feel strange," because their stomach was unsettled or they wondered if they had left a pot of beans boiling on the stove, and I would slip into that dream zone again and then have to claw my way back to reality. My entire drug career had lasted from age twelve to thirteen.

Mom was topless, her long batik skirt gathered around her thighs. She leaned back on her elbows, looking like a Maxfield Parrish painting. Ramón sat beside her and handed her the joint. I rummaged through the cooler and found an orange Fanta.

"How was your walk?" Mom asked.

"Good. I met this girl named Maria. Her grandpa owns the cantina down the beach. They invited us to come over and eat."

"Cool."

"Yeah."

Suddenly Ramón grabbed the baggie of dope and shoved it under the blanket. He stuffed my mom's bikini top into her hands and hissed, "Put this on."

As my mother fumbled with the strings, two federales came striding up the beach to our campsite.

"Qué es ésto?" the taller officer asked, turning back the edge of the blanket with the tip of his rifle and exposing the little plastic bag of weed.

"Oregano," said Ramón.

"Mota," the guy corrected him.

"No hablo español," said Ramón.

"Bullshit," said the officer. "Levántese. Venga conmigo."

But Ramón did not get up, and he did not go with them. He continued to cultivate a blank stare. The second guy tried to pull him to his feet. Ramón went limp. It was then that the fedarales noticed his miniature leg, and they looked at each other, momentarily confounded. I took this opportunity to throw myself at the feet of the first guy, wrap my arms around his knees, and beg him not to take my mama and my papa to jail. He ignored me. But a crowd of people had gathered around to watch the spectacle. They probably figured we had it coming, with our public nudity and flagrant drug use. I kind of thought so myself.

We spent the next hour locked in negotiations. Actually, I was the one doing all the negotiating. We had wordlessly agreed that my mother and her lover would feign illiteracy—even stupidity—while I would be the designated Spanish speaker.

And so I negotiated away all the money in Ramón's wallet and my mom's woven change purse. I negotiated away every last flake of their pot stash. And finally, when they were about to haul Ramón off to jail, I negotiated away his van.

They shouldn't have let me be in charge.

I should have let them take him.

●

In my explorations of the ex-patriot beach community, I had befriended Dick—a former insurance salesman from Indiana—a week or so earlier, who was renting an open-air palapa not far from our campsite. Dick had already become drinking buddies with Ramón (who dubbed him "Ricardo") and an obvious admirer of my mom. He paid attention to me, too, but not in a creepy way. He asked about my life back home in Taos, showed genuine interest in what I was reading, and brought me bags of fried pork rinds and Mexican chocolate bars from his beer runs to the village. Ricardo had one leg and one arm, as a result of a drunk driving accident years before.

But the most relevant fact was that Ricardo had an old white sedan he called "LaBelle Ford," and so I enlisted him to drive us home to Taos. He said it sounded like an adventure. We would leave at the end of the week. In the meantime, Ricardo would loan us a few bucks to get by.

That afternoon Ramón got drunk, picked a fight with Mom, and disappeared into the underbelly of San Blas. My mother responded by dropping the acid my father had given her, grabbing my hand, and running down the beach at sunset, leaping over driftwood and fire pits, her arms flung forward in a graceful arc, her legs thrust behind her like a modern dancer. I raced along beside her, trying to keep up. I couldn't. I let go of her hand and grabbed my knees, gasping for air. As the sky grew dark, her outline faded into the distance, and then she was gone.

Really gone. I could not see her. I could not hear her.

"Mom?"

No answer.

"Susy!"

From far below me, I heard a muffled cry. I scrambled to the edge of what turned out to be a bluff and peered down into the darkness. I could hear my mother's tiny whimper at the bottom of the cliff.

"Are you okay, Mom?"

"I think I've broken something."

"Wait. Don't move. I'll be right there."

And so commenced the longest night of my life. I scrambled down the embankment in the dark and managed to hoist my mother from the sand, thread her arm around my shoulder, and drag her, hopping, back up the bluff to the path that led to the cantina I had discovered a million years ago that week.

A string of Christmas lights lit up the outdoor tables and ranchero music blared from the speakers as we staggered onto the scene. Maria's grandfather came from behind the bar and took my mother's other arm. He led us to a table and pulled up a folding metal Dos Equis chair to prop Mom's rapidly swelling foot, which was also turning purple. I explained that my mother had fallen off a cliff and needed a doctor. He said we would not be able to reach anyone till morning, but we were welcome to spend the night in his bedroom behind the cantina, and he would sleep in his hammock on the beach.

Mom nodded, her face a veil of pain.

"Don Pancho, a sus ordenes." He extended his hand to my mom, who smiled as warmly as she could manage and returned his handshake.

"Susana. Mucho gusto."

"Come."

For the second time that day, we were the center of attention. All the drinkers had stopped drinking and the talkers had stopped talking. A dozen pairs of eyes followed us as we conveyed my broken mother through the bar. Don Pancho led us to his cement room beneath a thatched roof out back. The room was bare, except for a mattress on the floor, covered with a woven blanket, a shelf where he kept a couple of folded pairs of pants, and a rack with wooden dowels for an extra shirt and a spare straw hat.

My mom stretched out on the bed and winced. Then she bit her lip and moaned. I knew she must be in unbearable pain to be expressing anything at all. It almost seemed as if Matty's death had created an unspoken rule in our family that if you're not dying, you don't have a right to complain, because (according to family legend, anyway) Matty endured all those horrors and never even whined. Or maybe it was just that, for Mom, no mere physical discomfort was worthy of notice in comparison to the anguish of losing a child. But that night her customary dignity crumbled, and my mother began to quietly cry, lying on her back, the tears rolling down from the corners of eyes and dribbling into her hair.

I couldn't stand it. I ran out of the room and into the cantina. Don Pancho was standing behind the bar, mixing Cuba Libres. "Do you

35

have something for my mother to drink?" I asked. "Something to . . . help her sleep?"

The old man waggled his eyebrows, held up an index finger, and bent down. He emerged with a half a bottle of tequila. "This will knock her out." And he handed me the liquor with a wink.

Mom was not a drinker. I had to coax her to take a few sips, then a few more. It took hours to finish what was left in the bottle. In between, she would sleep fitfully, and just as I was drifting off myself, she would have to crawl out the door to the filthy outhouse behind the cantina and pee. I did not know there were so many hours in a night. Around a thousand, I think.

When the edges of the room finally began to turn gray, I leapt to my feet. "I'm going to find Ramón and Ricardo, and we'll get you out of here."

"Okay," Mom whispered. She was folded in herself, lying very still, as if she would shatter if she moved.

I tracked down the two hungover men, and we raced up the beach in LaBelle Ford to rescue my mom. Ricardo tried to pay don Pancho for his assistance, but the old man refused. He helped us load Mom into the car, kissed the top of her head, and asked God to bless us all. We spent the day in a dingy hospital in Tepic, where x-rays revealed multiple shattered bones in Mom's foot.

It no longer made sense to wait a week to head home to Taos. As soon as Mom's cast had set, we returned to Playa de los Cocos, packed our few possessions into Ricardo's car, and headed north. Ricardo, with his one leg and one arm, was the driver. Ramón, his polio leg locked in a brace, sat beside him in the front seat. Mom sat in the back with me, her broken foot resting in my lap.

LaBelle Ford was old. Her upholstery was torn, and the back passenger window was stuck halfway up, halfway down. This was fine for the first hundred miles or so, but after that the constant roaring wind began to give me a headache. That, plus the fact that by this time we had to ration our meager funds and so were subsisting on roasted peanuts and Coca Cola. Plus Ricardo was blasting Willie Nelson and Kris Kristofferson all through the Mexican countryside as we drove. And drove and drove.

Forty-eight hours later, we pulled up the driveway to our house in the valley of Valdez. I staggered out of the car, hungry, cold, disoriented as hell. Dad was standing in the doorway.

"Hi, Tootsie," he said to me, ignoring his ex-wife and her lover and our one-armed driver. He took my hand in his. "Come with me. There's something I need to tell you."

Dad led me inside, took me into Mom's bedroom, closed the door, and seated me on the edge of the bed. Then he knelt in front of me and looked into my eyes. I squirmed and looked away.

"Someone died," I whispered, heart pounding.

He nodded.

"Grandma?"

"Phillip."

"Phillip?"

"He was killed in a gun accident the day before yesterday."

"Gun accident?"

I don't remember what really happened next. If I collapsed in tears or narrowed my eyes at my father as if he was pulling my leg. If I pressed my dad for details or numbly nodded my head. What I do remember is that I grabbed a jacket and walked up to the road to hitchhike to Phillip's house. I needed to see Nora, Phillip's mom. I needed to see his sister, Zoe, and his brother, Eric, who were there when the 22-caliber rifle discharged at the prime angle. I needed my little sister, Amy, who had gone over to comfort her best friend.

By the time I was dropped off at the foot of Phillip's driveway, the sun was setting. Nora and the kids were just getting into the jeep to head to the Taos Plaza Theater where they were going to see The Ten Commandments. Like a zombie, I climbed into the back seat with the girls. Eric sat up front with his mom, and off we went.

No one spoke for a long time. Finally Zoe leaned over and whispered in my ear. "The day before Phillip died he had a dream. You were sitting behind him on his motorcycle, and he drove it really fast through the big window of his shed."

Thanks a lot, man, I muttered in silence. You left me to clean up the broken glass.

"This is for you." Zoe pulled a small sandalwood box out of her jacket. I opened it. In the light of the setting sun I saw Phillip's cherished thunderbird ring, inlaid with red coral. Zoe slipped it onto my middle finger and then handed me the box. My eyes filled with tears, and I leaned my head onto the shoulder of my boyfriend's little sister and shuddered with sobs. I was trying to cry quietly, because I didn't want to upset Phillip's mom. My own little sister grabbed my hand across Zoe's lap and held it tightly all the way to the theater.

I will save this ring until I am grown up and give it to the first guy I ever have sex with, I decided. It will be my virginity present.

This little pact with my dead first love brought me a certain comfort. I clung to that ring as if it were a life jacket tossed out to me as I bobbed alone in the middle of a stormy sea.

CHAPTER 6

Lama

While Mom was trying to fill her Matty-shaped emptiness with Ramón, Dad was slaking his thirst for their dead son with vats of cheap red wine and also some whisky. I burned alone in the fire of Phillip.

There may have been others who were incinerated by the death of my first love—his own mother and father, for instance; his sister and brother; his best friends, Hunter and David; and all the girls who wished he had been their boyfriend and maybe didn't understand why he would pick me—but no one spoke of him much. Or they only dropped small crumbs of memory here and there, as if by accident, which I snatched and gobbled, making a fool of myself. Wasn't anyone else starving for Phillip? People spoke sideways about death, heartbreak, about longing. I wanted a full-body encounter with the truth, even if it killed me. Especially if it killed me. Being dead seemed way more interesting than my messy little anguish.

Meanwhile, the dream that had caught me up in its clutches last spring kept dropping down and engulfing me. I would be in the middle of flipping french toast for Amy and Roy on a Sunday morning, and the smell of cinnamon would trigger the switch. Suddenly everything was lit up, as if a fire were burning holes in the fabric of the air, and I could see through to the other side—or tiny, fast-moving glimpses of the other world—much more real than this one. So real that my regular world was becoming the dreamscape, and I was trapped in between. I could not cross over to the true place, and I could never again believe in this one.

Purgatory—even more excruciating than loving a boy who was

dead, who died before I had the chance to make up with him, to wrap my arms around him and squeeze hard, to brush and braid his black hair down the long line of his rib cage, to try the whole giving-up-my-virginity thing again. This time I would not be such a baby. I would be brave and take him inside me.

•

Solitude was the only place where I did not feel lonely. I began to escape even more often than usual. I would grab my wool poncho, a jar of sweet mint tea, and my sketch pad and clamor down the path to the Hondo River with my dog, Sunshine, where I would set up a nest among the red willows and draw and sing the songs I was making up, over and over, until they were etched in me.

    The bells are tolling softly in the tower
    The snow is falling softly on his grave
    Now he's got a universe of power
    But we don't seem to see, not me, not even me

•

He used to tell me that he wished that he could fly
    Told me that there was an endless sky
    Told me that he wished he was a bird
    And now he's taken off without a word, without a word.

    Into the shattered cup of me a small light was beginning to seep, outlining the cracks, rising up to dampen the shards. I could only feel this delicate thing when I became very still, when I stopped singing and noticed the silence, when I set down my black felt-tip pen and looked up and out at the stream, when, exhausted by crying, I smelled the coming of spring and noticed the minute green shoots of riparian grasses sprinkling the loamy bank.

    The earth was slowly coming back to life. Actually, I hated that. I hated that the world went on without Phillip. That I too was expected to rise up and bloom.

•

In late May, after the Mirabai play, I moved up to the Lama Foundation and joined the summer staff. I was only fourteen, but I was determined to function as a full member of the team. My friend Margaret and her brothers and cousins grew up at Lama, but because their parents were the founders and they had already met every major spiritual teacher on the planet, they had cultivated the casual disregard of royalty and had no inclination to get up at sunrise and meditate with the self-important seekers who flocked up Lama Mountain as if it were Mecca.

I, on the other hand, sprang awake the moment the first bells—recycled warheads from the nearby Los Alamos labs—rang across the landscape and penetrated the dawn. I pulled on my cold clothes and headed to morning prayers. I signed up on the seva ("selfless service") wheel to feed the chickens and stock the outhouses with toilet paper, to cook gallons of black bean soup and fry dozens of tortillas, and to wipe the smudged globes of the kerosene lamps we used to illumine the dome at night when we chanted the ninety-nine names of Allah or conducted weekly business meetings. I wanted to be in the place where Mirabai had sung through me. I was showing up in case it might happen again.

•

That first summer I gathered the appropriate garments for my spiritual persona: drawstring muslin pants, fiesta skirts, hand-blocked Indian blouses and scarves. I fastened bangles on my ankles and wrapped a string of 108 sandalwood beads around my wrist. I draped my shoulders in a prayer shawl from Nepal, and I did not wear shoes. I read the collected works of Hazrat Inayat Khan and Carlos Castaneda. I memorized the Heart Sutra, and I observed three days of silence. There was not a spiritual practice I encountered that did not cause my heart to fly open and burst into flame. There was only one practice that filled me with fear: silent meditation.

The minute I settled onto my round black zafu and closed my eyes—
in the company of others or alone—the edges of my world swiftly lost
their shape and began to melt. Soon I would not remember who I was.
I could no longer feel the boundaries of my body. I'd lost all sense of
orientation in time and space. My breath grew shallow and almost
ceased. I could not have opened my eyes if I tried. I was being sucked
up and out and into the realm beyond this realm, about to hurtle off a
cliff into the void. It wasn't worth it.

No one else seemed to consider meditation to be a dangerous thing.
No one ever mentioned the perils of slipping into the abyss. They
blithely sat down, closed their eyes, and endured it for the requisite
thirty minutes, and when their time was up, they got on with their day,
washing dishes and thinning the lettuces, as if meditation were just
another task on the to-do list, rather than a brush with death. I carried
my secret like a glowing coal. Smoke came out of my ears. But the
adults around me—people in their twenties, mostly—had fires of their
own to hide. Like trying (and failing) to be celibate. Like not really
believing in God in a place where God was all anyone talked about.

●

Later that season, Ram Dass himself showed up at Lama, and I gave
up trying to keep myself grounded. Safe in his psychic embrace, I had
full license to blast off and away from the present moment. I finally
felt free to let the margins of my individuated consciousness dissolve
into the sky. Not only was I permitted to chant myself into a drunken
stupor, but that also seemed to be the point. This was the path of
Bhakti Yoga: lover disappearing into Beloved.

That was the first of several summers I served as Ram Dass's Lama
liaison. Every morning I appeared at his RV bearing sliced grapefruit
and a cup of black tea with milk, sugar, and ground cardamom. If
Ram Dass had wanted a newspaper and slippers, I would have gladly
delivered them in my mouth. I was smitten. I only wanted to make
him happy.

Ram Dass always asked how I was and inquired about my sadhana (spiritual practice), but I kept quiet, trying to be unobtrusive, finding out what he needed and then slipping away. I was proud of this, determined not to be needy, disdainful of the adults around me who were always clamoring for Ram Dass's attention.

Before Ram Dass came into the dome for his teachings each day, I would light the incense, wave it in front of Maharaj-ji's picture as I had seen others do, plump up Ram Dass's cushion, and straighten the Persian rug where he would be sitting. Then I would press my back against the adobe wall, close enough to respond if he needed anything, but far enough away to remain unnoticed.

Throughout those early years, I cultivated my invisibility, determined to eradicate my ego. The fact that I was too young to have had a chance to develop an ego escaped me, as did the fact that what little sense of self I might have managed to assemble was annihilated with Phillip's death when I was barely fourteen.

•

I began to assemble my spirit team. I set up a puja table in my tent: an aspen round that I covered with a mirrored cloth from India, on which I placed a small painted statue of Hanuman, the monkey god, incarnation of devotion; a wooden Buddha in seated meditation; and a brass Tara, Bodhisattva of compassion. Against this I leaned pictures of my team: Meher Baba, with his finger to his lips, admonishing silence; Maharaj-ji in his plaid blanket slipping into samadhi; Murshid Samuel Lewis leading Sufi dancing; and Joya, the embodiment of Kali, goddess of transformation.

But the most prominent deity on my altar was Krishna, Lord of Love, who had captured my heart, yes, and also absconded with it, leaving me ruptured and hemorrhaging. Krishna and Phillip took turns torturing me, and the truth was, I could no longer really tell them apart.

CHAPTER 7

The Guru and the Girl

That first year at Lama was not all about ecstatic states of consciousness and bonding with famous spiritual teachers. In between chanting the names of God and learning to bake bread, I was grieving. I staggered under the load of heartbreak: the death of my first love, the lack of empathy I was receiving over the death of my first love, the now long-ago death of my big brother, my parents' divorce and the reconfiguration of my family, my father's alcoholism and my new stepfather's alcoholism. Plus my propensity for spontaneous and debilitating hallucinogenic experiences, which made me feel like an extraterrestrial that did not belong on this planet. No one understood me.

Until Randy Sanders. Randy Sanders had moved from Southern California to Lama that spring with his wife and two children. His wife had a voice like Minnie Mouse and a tendency to see the world as a benign and uncomplicated place. His son was my age and his daughter a couple of years younger. Like most newcomers to the mountain, Family Sanders threw themselves into life at Lama. The wife became the "kitchen master," in charge of ordering bulk foods, stocking the underground root cellar, and planning menus for large groups. The son learned how to mix adobe plaster in a wheelbarrow and mud the cracks on the outside walls of the dome. The daughter convinced her elders to purchase white flour, sugar, and food coloring on town runs, and she baked and lavishly decorated cakes in the Lama's practically macrobiotic kitchen with recipes she found in The Joy of Cooking.

Randy Sanders strutted around dispensing spiritual teachings and making suggestions about community development. A middle-aged amateur scientist, he had greasy hair, pasty skin, a bulbous nose, and a potbelly. He bragged about everything, from the award-winning film he had supposedly produced on mitosis and meiosis to his scuba-diving instructor's certification to his association with Ram Dass to his gifts of clairvoyance. There was not a single lovely thing about Randy Sanders, except that he seemed to love me, and I was longing to be loved.

●

After ten years of running Da Nahazli, the alternative school in Taos, Tot's parents had given it up, and Lama had taken over. Asha, one of Lama's founders, was the new headmistress. Asha was one of the closest disciples of Murshid Sam, the Holy Fool Sufi master who invented the Dances of Universal Peace and proclaimed what I was beginning to suspect: all paths lead to the One. Up till now, Da Nahazli School only went through eighth grade, but there was a crop of us hippie kids between the ages of thirteen and fifteen who were dreading the prospect of public high school. That's where the "straight kids" went. We would never fit in. When newcomer Lama Bean Randy Sanders heard about this educational gap, he volunteered to start up a high school program at Da Nahazli for the coming school year. Asha was thrilled. Since I was one of the prime candidates for the new program, she made sure to introduce me Randy Sanders as soon as it was decided.

"I see you," he said. We were sitting on a bench under the Russian olive tree to become acquainted. He winked meaningfully. "You have hidden long enough. It's time to be who you are."

●

"I was there, you know. When she entered you. When you became her."

My head began to spin, and I thought I might shoot out of my body again.

Randy Sanders took my hand. "It's alright," he said. "We can take it slowly. You're not ready yet, but your time is coming."

Lama's summer program came to an end and it was time to head back down the mountain and home to my family, which had transformed into a circle of dangerous strangers. Mom and Ramón had bought a half-finished, half-underground, half-passive-solar house in Arroyo Hondo the year before, and they had been fixing it up ever since. They had brought back a pile of Zapotec rugs from a spontaneous road trip to a weaving village near Oaxaca in the spring, sold them all, and gone back for more. They convinced the owner of the ice cream parlor on the Taos Plaza to let them open a kiosk at the back of the shop, where they operated a thriving little import business. Now they had a home, a shop, and three children. But Ramón had not miraculously mutated into a family man. He still disliked kids. And Dad, who had moved into the one-room adobe shack on the hill above my mom's new house, did not seem to remember that we belonged to him.

Dad drank. And smoked—cigarettes and pot. Ramón smoked and drank too. Mom just smoked pot. No one talked about God. Or about feelings. The prevailing language of our extended family was sarcasm, and everyone seemed to have concluded that I was linguistically impaired. Whenever my feelings were hurt (every few minutes, it seemed) that was because I had no sense of humor. I was overly sensitive, too emotional, so dramatic. Always had been. Only I was worse now. Plus I had turned into a religious fanatic.

A Da Nahazli parent had contributed the building materials and blueprints for a one-room hogan—the octagonal structures common in Navajo country—so that our new high school program could have a room of its own. Randy Sanders was in charge of the building project. He tried to recruit parent-volunteers, but no one seemed interested in helping, so he spent the last few weeks of the summer banging it together by himself. When he invited students to spend a day organizing our new library from book donations, I signed up. Books were my thing.

My mother dropped me off at Da Nahazli on a Saturday in late August, promising to pick me up after she had finished the shopping and laundry. I expected a roomful of kids sorting novels and textbooks, but there was no one in the hogan except Randy Sanders. Inwardly groaning, I smiled politely and sat down cross-legged on the remnant of a beige shag rug covering the sand floor and began to pick through the pile of books: Findhorn Garden, Dune, Thirty Days to a More Powerful Vocabulary, The Tao Te Ching, Diet for a Small Planet; The Old Man and the Sea. Not bad. I could just read my way through the school year, read through my grief, read through the drunkenness of my two reluctant fathers.

"So." Randy Sanders said.

●

The next thing I knew, we were talking. About everything—about Phillip dying, about my mom running off with Ramón, about Krishna. One thing led to another and suddenly I found myself confessing my deepest secret: I told him about my altered states. I had not even been able to explain this syndrome to myself, and Randy Sanders got it right away! Not only did he grasp what I was saying, but he seemed to be familiar with the landscape I had been getting lost in. He knew the landmarks. He had navigational recommendations.

It turns out, he really did see me.

He saw that I was special and that my own family and friends did not recognize who I really was (a fact I had suspected for as long as I could remember). I was not only smart, but also probably a genius. I was almost unbearably beautiful. And, most relevant of all, I was a very high being on the brink of enlightenment. Randy Sanders offered to take me over the edge and then personally shepherd me through my full blossoming into an incarnation of the Divine Mother. In fact, this was most likely the reason he was born.

All I had to do was put my trust in him a hundred percent—nothing held back—and do exactly as he told me. Only my unconditional assent would open the gate to what was meant to be. What had to be. For the sake of all beings.

I took a deep breath and made the cosmic agreement.

•

The new school year began, and I took my place among a circle of eleven other hippie kids at the feet of Randy Sanders. I tried to be the perfect student to my new spiritual teacher disguised as my high school teacher. After all, the wellbeing of the whole world was balanced on my unquestioning surrender to his teachings. Randy Sanders described our connection as a vital energetic pole that maintained the balance of the universe. I was not about to mess with such a delicate and crucial mechanism. If he directed me to stay up all night chanting Hare Krishna and visualizing Randy Sanders, it was the least I could do.

But it wasn't easy. ("The way to God is not for the faint of heart," Randy Sanders would say.) Fasting was torture. By day two of ten I felt like I was going to throw up and pass out, and I wanted to kill someone. I would sneak sips of apple cider and handfuls of raisins and then beg for forgiveness. He assigned me "holy silence" exactly when my beloved grandmother was visiting from Miami, and she was not pleased when I pulled a little notebook out of my pouch and scribbled on it, "On silence. Please ask yes or no questions only."

Academically, it was not such a good fit. Randy Sanders was into math and science. I was a poet and an artist. Randy Sanders assigned us a weekly journal, in which he encouraged us to unburden our hearts and tell him everything. It would just be between Randy Sanders and each of us. Also, we should ask any questions we might have—from quantum physics to masturbation—and he would answer them all.

Not only did Randy Sanders address my most esoteric spiritual queries and write comments about how unconscious my various parents were, but he also got me to punctuate my poetry and hone my discursive language skills, which all my other Da Nahazli teachers had intentionally minimized in favor of unfettered creativity. On principle, for instance, I never capitalized my personal pronouns. Randy Sanders would patiently change all my lowercase I's to upper. I could understand making corrections like this on a punctuation exam, but in my journal? Randy Sanders explained that he was doing me a favor.

Another clash, one that unfolded on the secret battlefield of my own heart, was between Randy Sanders, our homeroom teacher, and Natalie Goldberg, our English teacher. This was connected to the math and science versus art and poetry issue. I don't think the two of them had any particular animosity toward each other—in fact, except as colleagues, they had pretty much a non-relationship—but I was torn between them at a very deep level. Natalie drew out my edge, my original and unconventional thoughts. Randy Sanders demanded purity and devotion. Where Natalie had been feeding me a feast of twentieth century women's literature (Ballad of a Sad Café, The Bell Jar, The Journals of Anaïs Nin), Randy Sanders insisted I read only "spiritual books" (Gesture of Balance, Autobiography of a Yogi, Mount Analogue). I found most of these to be dry and tedious, but, like sipping a bitter herbal tincture brewed to heal, I read every word, and my consciousness did begin to stir and stretch.

Tot and I used to buy half-sized spiral notebooks at El Mercado, the hardware store on Taos Plaza, and we would write together on the weekends and then read to each other—poems, short stories, song lyrics. By the time Randy Sanders came along, we had been keeping these "notebooks" for two years. Under the heat of Randy Sanders's disapproval, I stopped writing with Tot, confining all self-expression to my journal for Randy Sanders, which had shifted from a stream-of-consciousness flow to a serious exploration of the path of awakening. This writing was more of a dialog between Randy Sanders and me than a forum for my literary aspirations. Pretentions, Randy Sanders would call my dreams.

Natalie did not seem to notice that her most dedicated disciple was drifting away. She had matters of her own to grapple with: falling in love with a musician while simultaneously falling in love with Zen, making the Taos shift from earnest graduate student in English lit to hippie chick living in a house made from recycled beer cans on the mesa. Besides, we still met as a class twice a week beside the woodstove in the Da Nahazli hogan, where Natalie gave us wrinkled apples to eat from an orchard in Talpa and directed us to describe the images the experience evoked. She called these sessions "writing practice," which rendered it kosher for me. Writing practice as a spiritual exercise was preferable to writing as a worldly indulgence, which is the way Randy Sanders saw what it is I used to do.

Tot, on the other hand, was bewildered and heartsick. Her best friend was slipping away without a word of explanation.

"He has that girl in his clutches," Tot's mother, Naomi, told Tot, who told me.

I was furious. I stopped talking to Tot, my childhood soul mate. Randy Sanders approved.

After Christmas, Tot transferred to Taos Junior High, and I moved up to Lama full time.

●

Early that spring, Randy Sanders took our little group of twelve on a camping trip through the Southwest. We would be studying desert flora and fauna, geology and astronomy, Anasazi archaeology, and Ice Age paleontology. We would also be exploring the shamanic path of the native peoples, and must therefore (according to Randy Sanders), "be willing to leave behind everything we thought we knew."

To prepare me for the "inner plane" aspect of our expedition, Randy Sanders had assigned me to read A Separate Reality and Journey to Ixtlan by Carlos Castaneda, which described the author's spiritual adventures with don Juan, a Yaqui medicine man and enlightened trickster from the Sonoran Desert. The first night on the road, after a meal of hot dogs, Randy Sanders offered to walk me to my campsite. I ate carrots and potato chips for dinner. Randy Sanders had me on a vegetarian diet, so that my energy would be more "satvic," though he continued to eat meat himself, because it "grounded" him. (Otherwise, presumably, Randy Sanders would not be able to stay tethered to this material world. His soul was that elevated.) Earlier that day, soon after we pulled into the campground at Cochise's Stronghold in Southern Arizona and Randy Sanders had paid the ranger, he had guided me in selecting the place where I would sleep. He said that I was to walk around and find my "power spot" and that I would know it when I encountered it.

But I didn't. Each time I found a place that looked right, he would cross his arms and shake his head. I walked farther and farther from the center of camp, and Randy Sanders followed silently. Finally, I pointed to a secluded site between two granite boulders. Randy Sanders nodded and smiled. I felt a rush of pride, followed by dread. I did not want to be so far away from everyone else. I would be scared and lonely. A mountain lion might attack me. Or a wolf. But I could not admit this to Randy Sanders. I was in training as a "spiritual warrior," and this was my first real test.

After we had cleaned up from dinner, Randy Sanders handed me the flashlight and followed me as I endeavored to find the power spot I had located in the light of day. I crashed around amid the mesquite and ephedra, turning myself in helpless circles. I had absolutely no idea where my camping spot was.

"Feel it," Randy Sanders coaxed. But I could not feel a thing except a rising tide of panic. Finally I began to cry. Randy Sanders chuckled and took the flashlight from my hand. He led me right to the place where I had laid out my bedding. He patted my head, and feeling more like a puppy who had accidentally peed on the carpet than a shamanic apprentice, I untied my tennis shoes and climbed into my sleeping bag.

"Good night," Randy Sanders said.

"Good night."

•

It took me forever to fall asleep. I could not get warm. My down bag was thin and old. I'd found it in the Gypsy Wagon—Lama's free box—and my only jacket was an oversized fisherman's knit sweater I had inherited from one of my father's drinking buddies, which I wore to bed. The sweater was part of my image: it went down to my knees, and I had to roll up the sleeves a half a dozen times and still they reached my knuckles. The rest of my costume consisted of a floppy felt hat, moccasins from Taos Pueblo, strings of pooka shells and tiny brass bells, and a moon and star I drew with ballpoint pen on my forehead and also on the place where my thumb met the rest of my hand.

I tried to relax, but my mind had a mind of its own. I was sure I heard a bear snuffling in the bushes a few feet away. I had forgotten to stash my bag of dried apricots in the van with everyone else's snacks, as Randy Sanders had instructed. I was doomed. Finally, I must have drifted off, because I woke with a start. There was a creature crouched beside me, eyes glittering in the starlight. I leapt from my bed.

It was Randy Sanders.

"This is the hour of the saints and masters," he said. "Three a.m. The most potent time of day—a portal into other planes of existence—only most people are too lazy to stay awake, and so they forgo the opportunity."

"The opportunity for what?"

"You'll see. Sit down."

I obeyed. I grabbed my bag and wrapped it around my shoulders, then settled onto my threadbare InsuLite pad.

Randy Sanders guided me in a kundalini breathing practice. We started with slow, mindful breaths, in through the nose, out through the mouth. Then he directed me to close my mouth and just breathe through my nose in strong, sharp snorts.

"Faster! Faster!" Randy Sanders commanded. "Harder! Harder!"

I was breathing with all my might. I never knew such a natural function could be so difficult. Sparks began to shoot from the crown of my head. The ground was spinning in rhythm with my breath. I felt my body twisting on its axis—my left side turning one direction and my right side the other—but when I managed to open my eyes a slit and look down, I saw that I was sitting still. Suddenly my body went rigid. My hands contracted into claws, my toes curled, and my face contorted in a grimace. I could not move. I could not cry out.

"That's it." Randy Sanders's voice was far away. "Go up and out."

I tried. I tried to ascend through the layers of the material plane, to the astral plane, to the causal plane, as he had taught me. But it was hopeless. I was trapped in between the worlds, paralyzed, utterly inept. I had failed the most basic breathing practice.

When at last I could feel my body again, Randy Sanders was stroking my hair.

"There," he crooned. "Come back. It's time."

I tried to apologize, to ask him how I could do better next time, but all I could do was whimper. Randy Sanders took me in his arms and rocked me like a baby.

"Don't cry, Sweetpea," he said. Then he held me at arm's length. "You have no idea, do you?" He laughed. "You just made love to an angel."

                        •

The next night, I expected him. I lay awake in the dark and listened for his footsteps. It seemed as if he would never come, and I began to think my intuition was wrong. He had, after all, been paying a lot of attention to another girl that day. She was tall and dark skinned, poised and confident—everything I was not. She had been born in Europe, educated in Canada, had a boyfriend in his twenties. Randy Sanders seemed to be considering her as another disciple. I was trying not to feel jealous, but it was no use. How could I possibly compete with such exotic beauty and worldly wisdom?

Finally, I heard the approach of my master. Or a bobcat—I couldn't be sure. It was him! It was Randy Sanders! I sat up and almost sobbed in relief.

"May I?" he asked, indicating the ground beside me with the beam of his flashlight.

"Yes!"

Randy Sanders sat on his knees next to my sleeping bag. I reached out to hug him, but he shrugged away from me.

Oh no! He had switched his allegiance from me to the tall brown girl. Who could blame him? I was a shitty student. Not to mention short, and a little plump, with freckles all over my body.

Randy Sanders turned his head away from me in the darkness. I heard him breathing. His breath was shallow and rapid.

"Are you okay?" I asked, alarmed.

"Not really, no,"

"What's wrong?" I gripped my hands between my quivering thighs.

"I cannot be your teacher anymore."

"What? Why?" My heart was pounding. I felt like I would faint. Phillip's death was nothing in comparison to the prospect of Randy Sanders's abandonment.

He pulled out a rumpled pack of Camels and lit one with his Zippo. Cigarettes, too, grounded Randy Sanders. Without them, he informed us, he would not be able to stay in his body. This made sense, and we all nodded our heads.

"I have to confess something," Randy Sanders said, and he wedged the Camel between his teeth and took my hand in both of his, giving it a squeeze and then releasing. "I am attracted to you. It's getting in the way of our spiritual work. I have to let you go."

"No!" I shrieked.

"Shhh." He placed his hand on my mouth. It smelled like tobacco. Familiar, masculine, comforting.

"I don't care! It doesn't matter! You can still be my teacher. Please."

"You don't care? It doesn't matter? Well, thanks a lot." Randy Sanders chuckled, and I felt safe again.

I grabbed his arms and wrapped them around my shoulders, and snuggled against his chest. "Please don't give up on me," I whispered.

He hugged me back, his breath coming faster, his lips against my ear. "Okay," he said. "We'll give it a try."

CHAPTER 8

Deflowering

When we returned to Lama after the desert sojourn with Randy Sanders, we found that a foul-mouthed housewife from Brooklyn, purported to be an enlightened being, had infiltrated the spiritual landscape. Joya was being hailed as some kind of incarnation of Maharaj-ji, Ram Dass's beloved guru who had left his body a couple of years earlier. She seemed to be the new center of gravity in Ram Dass's world, and everyone around him tilted longingly toward her. Just as Ram Dass had drawn hundreds of seekers to India in search of Maharaj-ji, now the Maharaj-ji's Western devotees were flocking to New York in hopes that Joya would turn out to be him.

Joya had become accidentally awakened when she signed up for a weight-loss class and was practicing a yogic breathing technique on her bathroom floor several years earlier. Her third eye had sprung open, and there, sitting in lotus position on the toilet seat, was Jesus Christ, followed by Nityananda of Ganeshpuri, and finally the holy man Ram Dass had revealed in Be Here Now, Neem Karoli Baba. Since then, Joya was forever slipping into deep states of samadhi, punctuated by all kinds of iconoclastic antics, such as uttering streams of profanity at hapless chelas (devotees) seeking her darshan (spiritual transmission) and demanding that seekers bring her gifts of gold—to keep her connected to the earth plane—whenever they came to visit.

Randy Sanders invited me to join him and his family on a road trip back East that spring—a pilgrimage to sit at the feet of the Divine Mother.

"What about school?"

Randy Sanders looked at me sadly. "I guess your spiritual awakening is not as important to you as your mundane goals."

"It is!"

"Then be like Mirabai. Fling off your sandals and follow the sound of Krishna's flute."

Ram Dass wired a couple of hundred bucks so that the Family Sanders could make the journey from New Mexico. Although my parents were cynical about organized religion and considered the "guru trip" just another trap, they agreed that this could be a life-changing adventure for me. My father had heard good things about Hilda, the elderly white yogini who was said to be Joya's handler, and they trusted Ram Dass, who would be receiving us.

Randy Sanders struck them as harmless. He had a wife and children my age. I would be living with a family. Besides, they reasoned, I had always been wise beyond my years—at least since Matty died. I clearly knew what was best for me.

· · ·

The Family Sanders were dorks. I was constantly irritated with the wife, alternately attracted to and turned off by the son, and frustrated to be the object of continuous disdain by the daughter. Plus I yearned to be alone with Randy Sanders, so that we could get on with the urgent task of my awakening, and it was almost impossible to have him to myself.

I had no interest in being anyone's foster daughter. I did not mean to choose this awkward little family over my own. My family may have been fucked up, but they were interesting. So my father would shut himself up in his house with a fifth of something amber-colored and drink himself into oblivion every few days. He was a master of numerology, and the people of Taos revered him as a sage. So when Ramón would start drinking he would keep on drinking until his eyes glazed over, and then, with this x-ray psychic vision he seemed to develop once he had attained a certain level of drunkenness, he would see right into the most shameful part of my soul and expose it, and humiliate me in front of my friends. Maybe he was right. It certainly seemed likely to me that I was weak and pretentious. So my mother would not protect us against these slings and arrows. After having lost a child, what did we expect? Her heart was still broken.

●

It did not take long for Joya to kick us out.

When we arrived in New York, there was no room for a "family" of five in any of the communal houses in Brooklyn or Queens, and the cheapest apartment we could find was a one-bedroom flat on Staten Island. Every day we rode the ferry to Manhattan and took the subway to the various satsang houses where Joya gave darshan. Clutching our zafus, we would climb the stairs to some walk-up and cram into a room with the other Westerners dressed like Indians and then meditate until Joya made her entrance.

One day she swooped into the room, dressed in leopard-skin pants and a plunging bodysuit, flanked as usual by her entourage in their flowing Punjabi garb, and took her place on the dais built just for her. She scanned the room and her eyes landed on Randy Sanders.

"You!" she shouted, pointing a long red nail at him. Randy Sanders sat straighter on his cushion and tried to stare her down. "Don't bust my balls!" she said. "I'm not your goddam guru. Get out!"

And he did. He stood up and walked away. And we all followed: his goofy wife, his pious son, his rebellious daughter, and little lost me.

●

I drifted back across the country to California with Randy Sanders and his family. I had just turned fifteen—my first birthday away from my family—and I wasn't sure what to do next. In Napa we visited friends of the Family Sanders who, like my parents and their friends, had embraced a half-assed back-to-the-land lifestyle, which amounted a dash of voluntary poverty, a splash of psychedelic substances, and waterbeds nestled in the redwood forest. Upon one of these waterbeds

Randy Sanders continued my initiation.

It was late afternoon. The wife and son and daughter were grocery shopping in town. The couple whose property this was were making loud love in their yurt. Randy Sanders lay down beside me where I had been reading The Gospel of Sri Ramakrishna. He gazed deeply into my eyes.

"It's time for the next step of our journey together."

I began to tremble. The electricity was almost too intense to contain.

"Now kiss me. Take your time. Tune into our connection on all three planes."

Awkward, awe-struck, I kissed him.

"Use your tongue."

I inexplicably flashed on of my father. I accidentally pictured Ramón. I thought of middle-aged men in Coney Island hiking their swimming trunks over swollen bellies as they rose from their beach blankets to take a dip. I did not want to taste Randy Sanders's saliva. But I understood that my resistance was my doorway to transformation. I stuck my tongue into Randy Sanders's mouth. He moaned.

After a while of trying to figure out what to do with my mouth and how to coordinate my breathing, I felt Randy Sanders pull back from our embrace. "Now lie still."

He lifted my t-shirt and began to rub my belly. His hand ambled up to my breasts and his fingers lingered on my nipples, which had turned into pebbles. I gasped, squirmed. My eyes filled with tears.

"No," I whimpered. My body was on the verge of shattering into a million pieces.

"It's okay," Randy Sanders said. "It's just shakti, the energy of the universe. Let it take you." And he kissed me again, this time more slowly, and I surrendered.

Our final merging was yet to come. Randy Sanders promised that I would know when I was ready to fully receive him and be transfigured.

●

We spent the rest of the summer camping in the Pacific Northwest, and freeloading off various people the Family Sanders had met at Lama. I was beginning to despise myself. I kept falling apart. Messy emotional breakdowns. I could not articulate what was going on, and so Randy Sanders and his family put me in the center of a circle and held up their hands. They poured light from their fingertips, and I tried to let it wash over me as Randy Sanders instructed. His wife expressed her sympathy that I was having "such a hard time," and I wanted to slap her.

This technique of focusing on me and my problems did nothing to alleviate my frustration. It was not about anything they thought it was about. It was not some brokenness inside myself that tormented me. Not a matter of narcissistic obsession or thwarted desire. It was them. The Family Sanders were driving me crazy.

●

We were somewhere near the Oregon Coast, I think. There was a wide river, shallow and torpid, surrounded by towering Douglas fir trees. Randy Sanders splashed into the center of the river, and I followed him. We climbed onto a large flat rock. He took my hands.

"It is time for you to receive your spiritual name."

I did not want a spiritual name. Everyone I knew back at Lama had one, and I was embarrassed for them. Karima, Shanti, Wadud, Ganesh. As if having names in ancient languages would magically transform us into liberated souls. As if calling ourselves by the name of a goddess or a prophet made us automatically holy. Now, not only was I stuck with the Family Sanders, but I would also be saddled with an impossible-to-pronounce moniker. It would confirm my family's judgments about how I take myself too seriously.

He closed his eyes. I closed my eyes. "Your name is Mirabai."

My eyes flew open. Mirabai. That wasn't bad. I had carried the ecstatic poet saint inside me ever since playing her on stage at Lama after Phillip died. I had fallen in love with Krishna, and I still sang to him every morning when I woke and every night before I went to sleep: Sri Krishna, Govinda. I didn't even have to take on this name as a spiritual practice. Secretly I could consider it to be my nickname, springing from my role in a school musical.

Randy Sanders smiled. "I spoke to Ram Dass, and he sanctioned your naming. He sends you his blessings."

"Thank you," I said.

"Now memorize this moment. This rock, this river, my presence. This is your sacred touchstone. Whenever you need to remember who you are, close your eyes and come here. This place resides at the center of your heart."

·

Randy Sanders sent me home.

"You are too emotional," he explained. "It's starting to be a burden on our family."

Shamed, I boarded a Continental Trailways bus from San Jose to Albuquerque. Back home with my family, I was unmoored. I pined for Randy Sanders. Utterly bewildered by his rejection. He had opened a treasure trove of vital urgency, and then blithely snapped it shut.

I set up a tent at the top edge of my family's property on the other side of the irrigation ditch and tried to meditate, but the high desert sun beating on the nylon kept driving me out. I began to write poetry again and draw pictures of Krishna in my sketchbook. My heart stretched out toward the beautiful blue-skinned deity. "Come, my Beloved," I chanted.

But, just as the legendary Lord Krishna inflamed the hearts of the gopis with love-longing and then slipped away, the God of Love eluded me.

·

The school year was about to start, and I was facing either attending Taos High or dropping out at fifteen when the phone rang.

"Mirabai, it's for you!"

Mom did not seem to be having much trouble calling me by my

new name. "You feel like a Mirabai," she said. "Why should the name I gave you at birth have any more validity than the one you assumed?"

"I didn't assume it," I explained for the eleventh time. "It was given to me. It's my spiritual name."

"I see," she said. But she didn't. No one did.

It was Randy Sanders calling. Inviting me back.

The Family Sanders had decided to settle in Berkeley and wondered if I would like to come live with them and go to school there. Berkeley was famous for education. With a mind like mine, Randy Sanders concluded, the Taos school system would be travesty.

A flight of swallows exploded in my chest, and I left for California.

●

It was not easy leaving Amy and Roy. Sometimes they felt more like my children than my little brother and sister. I had groomed them in the mornings and gotten them ready for school. Cooked them grilled cheese sandwiches and rocked them after nightmares. Read to them and encouraged them to read.

Ramón was just as weird to them as he was to me, even if his weirdness took different forms. With me it was a laser-focused critique of my psyche, framed by eloquent flashes of sarcasm. For Roy it took the form of almost militaristic discipline, sometimes accompanied by blows when Roy talked back. Amy found her way by pretty much ignoring Ramón altogether. He didn't seem to know what to do with her quiet disdain, so he just ignored her back.

But there were other times Ramón was a like a giant stuffed animal come to life to cuddle and soothe us. Under the warm light of his love, all was well and always would be. Until he began to drink again and returned to his senses, remembering what little shits we actually were.

Mom was lost in love. Or lust. Or something we could not connect to. We missed her, but we had been missing her since Matty died and Roy was born and we cut the ropes that tied us to our life in New York and gone hurtling into space.

•

Randy Sanders kissed me and kissed me whenever the family was out. He massaged my breasts, guided my hand into his pants, whispered instructions for raising my kundalini.

"Are you ready?" he asked one day.

I nodded and reached for him.

"Not yet," he said. "Our time is coming. First you need to go home to Taos and make an appointment with Dr. what's-his-name for birth control."

"Michael."

Dr. Michael was our local hippie physician who presided over the free clinic in Ranchos.

"Okay," I said. But it wasn't okay. This plan felt like an almost unbearable ordeal. I dreaded going home to my family who, as Randy Sanders often pointed out, didn't get me at all and never would. The prospect of admitting to our doctor that I was about to become sexually active felt like confessing a mortal sin to a priest. But it was the next and highest step on my journey to awakening, and there was no turning back now.

"One more thing." Randy Sanders stroked my hair. "You cannot tell anyone that this is for me. Tell them you have decided to share your virginity with Barry." Barry was Randy Sanders's wife's brother's boy, and he was a fine-boned mulatto with bulging biceps. They had come over for dinner recently, and Barry and I had spent hours talking on the porch. He was a drummer, and we shared a love of music. Randy Sanders had forbidden me from continuing this mundane connection at the time, but now Barry came in handy.

"The world will not understand our love," Randy Sanders explained.

•

He picked me up at the bus station. The rest of the family was spending the weekend with his wife's parents, so we had the house to ourselves. Nevertheless, Randy Sanders had prepared a special nest for us in the garage. He led me through piles of gardening tools and abandoned croquet sets to a mattress surrounded by a wall of cardboard boxes, over which he had draped bolts of material from his wife's sewing collection.

He had arranged a circle of candles around the bed, which he now lit with his Zippo. From these small flames, he ignited a stick of jasmine incense, which he waved over the bed. His lips were moving in silent prayer.

"Now remove your clothing, beloved one," he said.

I stood before him, naked, shivering so hard I thought I would knock my own teeth out.

He stood before me and circled my body first with one of the candles and then the incense.

"Om Namah Shivaya," he chanted. "Jai jai Ma!"

•

After I gave Randy Sanders my virginity, I gave him Phillip's thunderbird ring. I had kept it inside the sandalwood box, keeping my promise to gift it to the first person I ever made love with.

But when I handed him the ring, along with a poetic prayer I wrote letting Phillip go, Randy Sanders handed it back to me as if I were trying to poison him.

"It's not appropriate to give me your dead boyfriend's things," he said. "Our love is not of this world. Don't you get it?"

No, not really. I didn't get it. There were so many rules, and they were not written down anywhere. I only learned them by stumbling over them, inevitably breaking something—something sacred and crucial and apparently irreplaceable.

•

I had to see Joya one more time. We heard that she was coming to the Oakland Hills to give a retreat at an old Boy Scout camp, so I signed up for a scholarship and got it.

Randy Sanders was not pleased, but he shrugged his shoulders. "You will have to discover for yourself that painted cakes do not bring satisfaction," he said, quoting from Be Here Now. "There are false teachers and there are true teachers," he went on. "The former will betray you, and the latter will set you free."

"But I didn't get to say goodbye to her. I just want to say goodbye."

It turned out, as Randy Sanders had predicted, to be a colossal mistake.

On the first day we gathered in a meadow and waited. It was a hot autumn afternoon, and there was no shade. Finally, the guru sashayed onto the scene wearing a purple bikini. Her Mediterranean complexion glistened with baby oil. She settled onto her pile of cushions and closed her eyes, appearing to slip effortlessly into a deep trance. We sat in silence. The air pulsated with power.

When Joya opened her eyes, she called for me. "Where's the fifteen-year-old brat?"

I looked around, schizophrenically praying it wasn't me she was summoning, and craving her attention with all my heart. She was staring at me through the crowd. I rose and went to her.

"Come, baby," she said. "Sit in my lap."

"Ma, Ma," the assembly murmured.

Joya wrapped her arms around me and rocked me. I began to cry. She nuzzled my face with her face and hummed "Bridge Over Troubled Waters."

"Where's your mommy, Honey?"

I ignored the question, inhaled the fragrance of her neck, a blend of Nagchampa and coconut.

One of Joya's attendants leaned over to explain that I was here on my own.

"What? Does your mother know where you are?"

"It doesn't matter," I whispered.

"Speak up!"

"She doesn't care."

"That's what you think," Joya said. "A mother always cares. That's all mothers do is care." And she swept her gaze over the crowd of worshippers.

"Are you a virgin, kid?" she suddenly asked.

I flushed, squirmed, kept quiet.

Joya pushed me out of her arms and held my face between her hands. "You don't understand the question? Cherry! Has anyone popped your cherry?"

This was way too complicated to address with a simple yes or no. I could not consider what I had done with Randy Sanders a question of virginity. It was a cosmic rendezvous that altered the gravitational field the earth itself.

"Get over here." Joya snapped her fingers at her handsome son—a guy in his early twenties who drove a motorcycle. "Take her into the bushes over there and talk some sense into her." He rose and reached out his hand to me. I shook my head hard.

"So you don't like them young?" Joya said. "Okay. You!" And she beckoned a balding man with a thin gray beard, who came over and lifted me to my feet.

I didn't feel like I could refuse the Divine Mother a second time, so I went with him, reinforcing the notion that I preferred older men. I chafed against the irony of my predicament and trailed behind him to an oak grove, where we sat across from each other and stared into each other's eyes for as long as I could stand it.

●

That night we all chanted in the main hall.

"Call out to God," Joya coaxed from her place at the head of the room, flanked by musical devotees playing harmonium, tablas, and small brass cymbals. The Brooklyn housewife had morphed into the goddess and sublime poetry flowed spontaneously from her lips. "However you most deeply connect to the Divine, my children, visualize that, manifest that, merge with that!"

With every fiber of my being I called Krishna's name.

And he came to me. In spite of Randy Sanders, even in spite of Joya, independent of every spiritual book I had read and every spiritual teacher at whose feet I had prostrated myself, my Beloved came flooding into the shattered container of my heart and filled me with even greater longing. I sang to him, I wept, and I sang some more.

●

Eight years later I married Randy Sanders. Eight years after that, I left him. The sky, just as he had predicted, fell. And the whole world opened to receive me.

Part 2

CHAPTER 9

Daniela

I did not give birth to my children. But I poured every particle of my maternal juices into loving them.

It all started when I was sixteen and, convinced that the planet was hurtling toward environmental devastation, I vowed that I would never bring children into this world.

I had followed the Family Sanders to the Mendocino Coast, where they had been offered a job caretaking a farm near Albion. We were raising chickens and goats, building berms around the vegetable gardens to block the coastal gales, experimenting with windmills to pump water and solar panels to heat it. Randy Sanders's vision was to create a community over which he would preside with spiritual rigor and common sense.

I dropped out of school, then hooked up with an alternative program designed for teenagers living on their own. I passed the California High School Proficiency Examination and enrolled in classes at the local community college. Like my father before me, I jotted enthusiastic notes to myself in the margins of my favorite new books: Small Is Beautiful, Pilgrim at Tinkers Creek, Desert Solitaire, Of Wolves and Men. I studied classical choral music and South Indian dance, creative writing and astronomy, and a new multidisciplinary course called "Futuristics," which combined sociology, philosophy, economics, and environmental sciences. This was the seventies, and the hot-button issue was overpopulation. It seemed self-evident that if everyone were to carry on reproducing with abandon, humanity would implode and become extinct within a hundred years.

I, for one, was not about to contribute to the crisis. If I ever had the overwhelming urge to bear a child (which seemed unlikely), I would adopt one. And not some blond-haired, blue-eyed infant, but an older child, preferably black, possibly with a serious physical or mental handicap, maybe even terminally ill. I couldn't understand why everyone didn't feel the same way.

Hooking into the same determination with which I eventually gritted my teeth and married Randy Sanders at age twenty-three, I found myself at twenty-eight the mother of an eleven-year-old girl named Daniela.

When I married Randy Sanders, I had supported his plan to have a vasectomy. Randy Sanders had two grown children at that point and no interest in bringing up another baby. Elated to be with him out in the open after years of secret love, I tried to repress the longing for a baby that was rising inside me. My breasts ached to suckle an infant. Every time I passed the midwifery center on my way to the grocery store, my eyes filled with tears.

A local Taos doctor and his wife had founded a special needs adoption agency, and I convinced Randy Sanders to meet with them and explore the possibility of fulfilling my youthful vow to take on a child society had thrown away. We sat in the agency office, leafing through loose-leaf binders with photocopies of children's faces and short descriptions beneath them: "Joseph (prefers to be called 'Joey') is a handsome nine-year-old boy, part African-American, who was born with a heart defect. This does not slow him down much! Joey enjoys throwing a football with his foster father. He wants to grow up to be a pilot in the air force." And "Juanita is a quiet girl of seven who does not yet speak but would likely flourish in a family with several other children." And "Although the right placement has not yet been found for Jason, an energetic boy of twelve who has been in the system since birth, we feel he would be the ideal fit for a retired couple who can devote the majority of their time to nurturing this special young man."

Every page battered down the doors of my heart. Every child felt like my child. Each time I moved on from one to another it was as if I were single-handedly condemning another soul to Purgatory. In despair, I closed the book and took Randy Sanders's hand. I shook my head, and we left the office. That night, the phone rang. It was the adoption agency.

"We have just heard about a child who was not in the book," the social worker said. "We think she might be just right for you."

The next day Randy Sanders and I drove back to the agency, where they showed us a picture of a ten-year-old girl with close cropped black curls and cappuccino skin. Daniela's biological father was a Hell's Angel from Puerto Rico, and her biological mother was a biker chick from North Dakota. The dad was long gone, and the mom had since given birth to three other children by three other fathers. Daniela was the only one of mixed race, and she did not blend well into the ultra-white world of the Midwest. Her mother gravitated toward abusive relationships, which eventually caught the attention of Child Protective Services.

Between the ages of six and eleven, Daniela had bounced from foster home to foster home, and endured one disrupted adoption, before that day in Taos when we sat in front of the social worker and said we'd think about it. Which meant, of course, yes. This was not a cattle auction. I was not about to inspect her teeth and squeeze her flanks. This was a child. And she needed us. Obviously it was meant to be.

We drove up to South Dakota and met Daniela just after her eleventh birthday. A week later we brought her home.

And a couple of years after that, I left Randy Sanders.

●

When Daniela was sixteen, she graduated from high school early and fled to South Dakota to live with her birth mom (the Other Mother), who had not miraculously transformed into a healthy parent ready to make up for lost time. The Other Mother's three other children had also been taken from her, and she was still choosing abusive men. Playing on Daniela's victim conditioning, she convinced our daughter that I was a selfish bitch and she should cut all ties with me. Daniela and I did have a stormy relationship, and I was relieved to have a little break. But I did not want it to be forever, and I pined for my first child.

The trouble was, I had adopted Daniela at exactly the age when a child begins the requisite individuation process. So we were bonding and unbonding at the same time. It was confusing for us both. Plus, attachment to any adult had proven to Daniela to be a risk not worth taking. After being shuffled from family to family for more than half her young life, Daniela was finally placed in what she was told would be a forever family. And then, before she could grow out her hair, I had left the only father she ever knew and all my attention was going to her new four-year-old sister, Jenny. My efforts at single-parenting a rebellious teenager were haphazard and half-hearted. I knew she was partying and probably having sex, but I felt powerless to keep her home.

Daniela's new boyfriend, a transient from the East Coast, who had been in and out of prison since his teens, followed her to South Dakota. When Daniela discovered she was pregnant, growing tension between her and the Other Mother escalated into a harrowing fight. Daniela called me crying so hard she could not speak.

"Mom, I'm pregnant," she finally blurted out. "Can I come home?"

Now I was crying too. "Yes, my love, come home. I'll send you a ticket."

A week later I was sitting on my knees beside the tub while my daughter lay in the warm water, her belly rising like a mountain amid the great hills of her breasts, and I was singing to her unborn child.

Gopala, Gopala, Devaki Anandana Gopala. Oh sweet baby Krishna, bliss of your mother.

●

Jacob was born on the spring equinox. I was thirty-six years old, and my new spiritual name was Grandma.

Daniela applied for a job at the local nursing home and rented a place with the father of her baby. When Jacob was six months old, I was in Mexico teaching a writing workshop, and Daniela was housesitting for me. She decided to seize the opportunity to leave Jacob's father, who had become increasingly jealous and violent. One afternoon he came over, snatched the axe from my woodpile, broke into the house, and accused Daniela of cheating on him. He smashed her face with the axe handle. Then he grabbed her by the hair and dragged her into his truck, where he slammed her head against the window and drove away with her. He took her to a trailer on the south side of town and locked her and the baby inside. Jacob inexplicably slept through the whole thing.

A neighbor who heard the commotion called the police. Daniela went to the hospital, Jacob went to my mom's, and his father went back to prison. I caught the next flight home from Cancun.

Next, Daniela moved in with a manic auto mechanic who treated my baby grandson as an intruder. Although he was only five years my junior, this one called me "Mom." While I was busy praying my daughter would come to her senses and hook up with someone sane, Daniela discovered she was pregnant again.

"Didn't you teach her about birth control?" a well-meaning relative by marriage asked me once.

"Good idea," I said. "Why didn't I think of that?"

Bree was born a week after Jacob's second birthday.

Niko came along four years after Bree.

Like lotuses, these three beings rose up from the brokenness of Daniela's life and transfigured us all.

CHAPTER 10

Jenny

Two years after Daniela had come to live with us, I was still with Randy Sanders, and I still wanted a baby.

I did not want to want a baby, but adopting Daniela had not made the yearning go away. Throughout my relationship with Randy Sanders, I was always secretly falling in love with other men. There were, I think, a few reasons for this: one is that Randy Sanders had conditioned me to believe that true love was clandestine affair, and another was that my body craved the body of someone my own age with whom I could reproduce. Not to mention that I was not sexually attracted to Randy Sanders and never had been.

Like a wizard, he had spun such a powerful spell over me that I forsook the family I loved and the boys I had crushes on for the promise of enlightenment and the threat of being responsible for unraveling the fabric of the universe if I were turn one iota away from our Great Love. As the years went by, our life together lost its spiritual dazzle but grew comfortable, even comforting, and I was determined to prove to the world that I had grown into Randy Sanders. Grown worthy of him.

Not long after we brought Daniela home, I fell in love with Jonathan. Randy Sanders and I had taken over the defunct New Buffalo commune and turned it into an alternative high school for gifted adolescents. The entire facility was made of mud, and after several years of not being lived in, it had begun to return to the earth from whence it came. We moved into one of the smaller buildings with our new daughter, while converting the numerous adobe cells into classrooms and the Great Buffalo Room into our common meeting space. The families of our twelve students helped in the reconstruction project—often in exchange for tuition—and I worked nights as a cocktail waitress at Ogelvie's Bar and Grill to pay the bills.

Jonathan was in transition. He had been living at Lama and was now ready for the next step, but didn't yet know exactly what that would be. We offered him a space at New Buffalo while he sorted out his life, and he helped with maintenance. Jonathan was dark and muscular, funny and Jewish—everything Randy Sanders was not—and he was age appropriate. He had the soul of a poet, and he sang kirtan. His genetic code resonated with mine. And his spiritual fire matched my own. Unlike Randy Sanders, whose self-importance was beginning to embarrass me, Jonathan didn't put himself forth as some kind of rarified being. Jonathan's humility made his singularity all the more luminous.

My previous crushes had sparked and then faded away, flared up dramatically and quietly subsided, seemed at first like something uncontrollable and then turned out to be forgettable. But with Jonathan it was different. My desire for him only intensified. It was torture watching him bustling around the property, weeding the grass on the living roof of the Great Buffalo Room, chopping wood to feed the potbelly stoves my mom had donated for the classrooms, making tea in the communal kitchen, and then sitting down with the poetry of Sharon Olds while he sipped it. I was convinced that Jonathan was the prefect partner for me. But my vow to Randy Sanders was inviolable.

At first I kept my feelings to myself. Even Jonathan did not seem to suspect. I longed to confess my attraction but was terrified of the consequences. I wasn't sure which prospect was more dreadful: destroying my family or finding out that Jonathan did not reciprocate my affection. Then I had an idea: I would ask Randy Sanders if I could have a baby with Jonathan. That way, I could stay true to my marriage, satisfy my desire for a baby, and always have Jonathan in my life.

I used this plan as a pretext for approaching Jonathan.

He was flattered by my interest, but he did not see me "that way." I was a married woman with a preteen daughter, the headmistress of a school, a pillar of the community. Besides, he wasn't interested in sharing a child with another man. If he were ever to have kids, he would like to raise them himself. I had to admit, he had a point. It wasn't like I was offering myself as his devoted mate. I was asking him to impregnate me and then hand over the fruit of our union. Still, he said he'd think about it. This sliver of hope was enough for me. The cart had been pushed into motion, and I let the momentum carry me. I took the next step and proposed the arrangement to Randy Sanders.

He must have sensed that I was starting to slip away from him, because he quickly came up with an alternative plan. He nixed Jonathan as sperm donor, on the sensible grounds that if I were to have sex with him I might fall in love with him, and he suggested Michael instead. Michael was an old friend from Lama who now ran a successful city-planning firm in San Francisco. Michael had always been like a brother to me and seemed safe to Randy Sanders. He was good looking, but had proven to be just goofy enough to preclude my being suddenly swept away by his charms after all these years. Plus Michael was in a better position to provide for his baby, which appealed to Randy Sanders as a supplemental source of income. Randy Sanders called Michael and reported back: he too would think about it.

But I didn't want Michael's baby. I wanted Jonathan's baby. What I really wanted was Jonathan.

●

"What if we adopt another child?" Randy Sanders randomly suggested one evening as we were washing the dinner dishes. "We could find a younger one this time."

"Another child? You up for that?" I asked.

Randy Sanders was obsessed with Daniela, scrutinizing her every move and correcting her attitude at every turn, and I knew it was stressful for him being a parent again after thinking he had long ago checked that item off his list.

"As long as it's old enough to be in school so we have that break during the day," he said. "And . . . I know you you're not satisfied."

I couldn't tell if he meant satisfied with my life, satisfied that our family was complete, or maybe even sexually satisfied. He would be right on every count. But after so many years of being conditioned to believe that the cosmic balance hung on my devotion to Randy Sanders, I could never admit this. Not to him, not to myself.

"What are you talking about?" I squeaked. "I'm totally content." And I threw myself in his arms to prove it, pressing my body against his.

Daniela pushed open the door to the kitchen, and I sprang back. "Mom, can I have dessert now? I finished my algebra." Without waiting for a response, she reached on top of the refrigerator for the plate of brownies I had stashed there.

Daniela had called us Mom and Dad right from the beginning. Having lived in eleven foster homes in eleven years, she was ready to settle down—even if her new mother was young enough to be her sister and her father old enough to be her grandpa. At thirteen, Daniela was already taller than me (which was not saying much; I'm barely five feet tall), and she outweighed my by around ten pounds. Temperamentally, we bewildered each other. Where at her age I had been drawing mandalas and reading the Beat poets, Daniela liked to sing commercial jingles from the days when she lived in a house with television, and seemed unable to differentiate between the value of a handcrafted turquoise ring from my mother's folk-art collection and a rhinestone pendant from K-Mart. But we were all making the best of our odd little configuration. Maybe a fourth person would alleviate the pressure, shift some of Randy Sanders's attention off Daniela, and allow me to baby someone with impunity.

"Hey, Daniela, want a little brother?" Randy Sanders said, draining his last can of beer.

My heart raced. If he was bringing this up with our daughter, didn't that mean we had to follow through? We couldn't dangle such a thing and then pull it back. It would be devastating for a child whose entire early life had unfolded on an open battlefield of emotional assaults.

"Or sister!" she said. "Can I have a baby sister?" She grabbed my hands, yanked hard, snapping my head on my neck. "Please, Mom?"

Randy Sanders chuckled. I stared at him, then turned back to

Daniela. "We're thinking about it, Honey."

"Yay!" She threw her arms around me. "This will be so cool."

●

"This one's a full hand," our Portuguese social worker told us when she came over and laid out pictures of our new daughter. "But I think you can handle."

A week later, we met Jenny at her foster home in Albuquerque and took her to the zoo. It was my thirtieth birthday. Two weeks after that, Jenny's social worker met us at the Dunkin Donuts in Santa Fe with a paper bag containing all Jenny's worldly belongings, and we brought her home. It was Mother's Day.

Jenny was four years old, but she looked like two-and-a-half. She was spindly and weightless, and when I lifted her into my arms her limbs dangled like a spider's. She barely spoke, and when she did her voice was creaky and her syntax bizarre. Jenny had the most exquisite face I had ever seen on anyone of any age: enormous black eyes, perfectly arched brows, a mouth like a peony bud, flowing black curls, and luminous brown skin. All I wanted to do was carry her around on my hip. And all Jenny wanted was for me to carry her.

I finished out the school year taking Jenny with me to classes. She sat at my desk and colored while I led my students in creative writing exercises and taught them to conjugate Spanish verbs. Jenny was quiet and undemanding. She rarely smiled. There was a certain dignity and reserve about this tiny girl that seemed to intimidate older people, as if she saw into their souls and was not at all sure she approved of what she perceived there.

One day after school, as I sat at my desk grading papers, Jenny stood behind me drawing on the chalkboard. When I finally swiveled in my chair to check out her artwork, I saw a female form with a bulging belly, inside of which nestled a smaller version of the same figure.

"What's this, sweetie?"

"That's you," Jenny said. "With me inside your belly."

My daughter was reinventing her history before my eyes. And I liked it.

•

When Jenny was around seven, we were driving home from school, and I heard her sniffling beside me. I turned to see tears streaming down her cheeks. Her shoulders were shuddering with silent sobs.

"Jenny, what's wrong?" We were heading down the Hondo Hill into the valley. I stroked Jenny's long black curls with one hand and steered with the other.

"I don't want you to die!" she wailed.

"Honey, why are worrying about that?" But Jenny was crying too hard to answer.

I pulled over to the side of the road, lifted my daughter over the gearshift, and wriggled her into my arms. I did not ask any more questions. I just held her head against my breast as she sobbed.

Finally, she quieted and looked up at me. She lifted her small hand to stroke my cheek. "I was looking out the window," she explained, "and I saw some trash on the side of the road. I thought, "My mom loves Mother Earth. What if she stopped the car to pick up that trash, and a big truck came along and ran her over?"

Recounting this imagined scenario sent Jenny into a fresh round of crying. I squeezed her and rocked her and crooned to her until she could breathe again. By which time I was breathless myself. I had never been so fiercely loved in my life.

CHAPTER 11

My Father in the Mirror

Nine months after we brought Jenny home, I vaulted off the cliff and left Randy Sanders to be with Jonathan. But Jonathan was not waiting with a safety net as he had promised.

"What happened?" I asked, blinking in disbelief, clutching one little girl by the hand while the older one sat apart, fuming.

"I need some time," Jonathan said. "And you do too."

•

As I tumbled from the sky, Jonathan's friend, Michael Two, swooped in and scooped me up. The only reasonable response was to sleep with him. Having been with Randy Sanders from age fifteen to thirty-one, I had lost time to make up for, and Michael Two was famous for his sexual proficiency. But the next thing I knew, Michael Two was moving in with me. He was fun to be with, but he was not my beloved. There was only one person formed in the exact shape to fit my exact shape, and he was not even returning my phone calls. So I girded my loins and tried to love Michael Two the best I could.

Meanwhile, Randy Sanders spiraled into an alcoholic mania. He smashed the wall of south-facing windows in our passive solar house while we were camping in the Gila Wilderness, claimed to have swallowed a lethal dose of pills several times a week and then hid under the porch when the paramedics came to fetch him, and custom designed curses for Jonathan and me. Mine was: you will never have a baby. Jonathan's was: you will not be with Mirabai, and you will never find happiness with anyone else.

One day Michael Two and I drove to the airport in Albuquerque to drop off his daughter, who had been visiting for the summer from Southern California. My mother had booked a room for us at a bed-and-breakfast in Old Town, arranged a gift certificate for an Italian restaurant on the Plaza, and took the girls for the night. I needed a break, and Mom knew it. Between my ex-husband's violent shenanigans, the abandonment by the love of my life, my accidental domestic arrangement with Michael Two, and finding my way as a single parent of two daughters with special needs, I was friable. I had dipped below ninety pounds, which satisfied the old anorexic in me but horrified my family, who tried in vain to ply me with lox and bagels.

I could not choke down our fancy dinner out that night and made Michael Two eat my fettuccine alfredo. Back at our hotel room, we made love with the TV on. Afterwards, I went into the bathroom and took a look at my naked self in the mirror. But it was not my jutting clavicle that drew my attention; it was my face. A terrifying radiance emanated from it. I had never seen such beauty, and I gasped, as if I were encountering a beautiful other. I met her eyes with my eyes, and we gazed lovingly at each other for a while. When I lay down to sleep, I rested more deeply than I had in my whole life.

●

The next morning, Michael Two and I went to Corrales to have brunch with Charlene, my mentor from graduate school and the godmother of my daughters. Charlene was brilliant and hilarious. She had earned three PhDs by the time she was twenty-two: one in mathematics, one in physics, and the other in philosophy, but she was the humblest and quirkiest person I knew. She modeled to me that a permeable heart and a finely tuned brain are not mutually exclusive, and she freed me to express myself in hyperbole. We were physical opposites. Charlene was Sicilian, with lanky limbs, a halo of black curls, and an olive complexion always perfectly enhanced with red lipstick.

Charlene greeted us at the door of the house she shared with her husband, Kevin and swept me into her bony embrace. Then she suggested I call home.

"What? Why?" I asked. Kevin handed me a cup of coffee with a sad smile.

"Is it my father?"

Charlene nodded, took my other arm, and led me to her study.

Dad had been diagnosed with prostate cancer a few months before I left Randy Sanders. The year before that, he had moved his widowed mother from Miami and taken care of her until she died a few months later. Living with an elderly Jewish princess with growing dementia was not easy for a curmudgeon like my father, but he galvanized his team and did the best he could to feed and dress and entertain her. Within months of Grandma's death, Dad found out he was sick. While I was navigating the tumultuous seas of my divorce, my father had been dancing with his mortality. True to his drunken-poet lineage, Dad had embraced his cancer as a troubling but interesting new friend.

"It's an adventure, Cookie," he assured me.

Lately, he had been resting more. After his surgery and radiation, Dad had enjoyed six months of relative good health, during which he flew to Las Vegas and played in his first Bridge tournament since we had left New York. He had also accompanied Mom and Ramón to the Yucatan, where he stayed with them in their winter home on Laguna Bacalar, swimming every day in the Lake of the Seven Blues. My mother and her lover had taken on the details of my father's care, coordinating medical appointments and researching complimentary alternative therapies. But recently, the cancer had come back, and Dad was trying to decide what he wanted to do next.

What he did next was die.

●

Instead of calling my mother, I dialed my father's apartment, and Mom answered.

"Mom? Is Dad okay?"

"He's gone, my love."

Wait! We had not had time to plan a good death. He was not even bedridden yet. Only last week he mentioned to me that maybe I should call a few of his old friends and ask them to stop by and visit. He was lying on the couch in his apartment with a Pall Mall in his hand and an ashtray on his belly. I curled up beside him in an overstuffed chair and met him in the growing silence. He kept drifting off and then opening his eyes and gazing around with a puzzled expression. I had been watching his cigarette burn down low between his fingers, and I finally slid it from his hand and stubbed it out.

"I have been visiting the other world, Cookie, and I have to tell you, it's much more real than this one."

Now he had crossed that boundary, and this time he was not coming back.

My mother murmured soothingly into the phone. She told me that his friend Karim had come over to watch football game with my dad and ended up washing his body instead, along with my brother, Roy, who had been tending our father all summer. Mom assured me they would keep Dad's body in his bed until I could get there to say goodbye.

"I'll be home in three hours," I said and hung up.

In the pulsing silence of Charlene's office, I wrapped my arms around my own chest and spun in a slow circle in her swivel chair. Suddenly, it was my father's arms cradling me. Holding me as he never been comfortable enough in his own skin to hold me in real life. Comforting me, keeping me safe. I let myself down into his embrace.

"Oh Daddy," I whispered.

It was only later, as I sat in silence while Michael Two drove me home, that I remembered my encounter with the beautiful being in the mirror the night before. I realized this had been my father coming to say goodbye.

CHAPTER 12

Monkey Temple

When I left Randy Sanders, I fired God. Every aspect of my spiritual life had been shaped by my association with an imposter. Suspicious of anything resembling an organized belief system, all the teachings I had once embraced I now dismissed as artifacts of magical thinking. My parents, Freud, and Marx were right: religion was the opiate of the masses, and my addiction had almost killed me. It was time to sober up.

I quit reading spiritual books. I stopped going up to Lama for Shabbat and zikr (Sufi chanting). I took down most of my pictures of saints and deities, and I stashed my statues of the goddesses and Buddha in the closet. I gave away my Jai Gopal and Sufi Choir cassettes, and I made fun of the people I knew who flocked to convention centers to get hugged by the Hugging Saint or take the Bodhisattva Vow. I didn't give up my basic hatha yoga practice, because I had been doing the sun salutations almost every morning of my life since I was fourteen, and the cells of my body had formed around those movements. I also maintained a silent sitting meditation practice because I noticed that when I didn't, I had more of a tendency to yell at my children for no good reason.

I endeavored to replace my spiritual escapades with sex, drugs, and rock-and-roll. Well, maybe not drugs—I still had a propensity for slipping into altered states, and so I wasn't interested in anything more than a glass of red wine with dinner—but I did dabble in sex. My relationship with Michael Two lasted less than a year, and I went on to experiment with a variety of flavors of men, rebuilding what Randy

Sanders had destroyed. I quickly discovered that I could not keep my heart out of the equation, and so, after sleeping with a few men who, to my surprise, did not want to spend the rest of their lives adoring me, I decided to be more discerning.

My closest friend was our next-door-neighbor on the Hondo Mesa—a singer-songwriter named Jenny Bird. It is true that she had an inclination toward the spiritual life, but I did my best to change the subject whenever she spoke of such things, shifting the focus back to music (or sex). I became Jenny Bird's road manager and spent a few euphoric months as the girlfriend of her bass player. When the Beautiful Bass Player—who was too creative to hold down a job and so relied on me, a struggling single mother, for support—began to act more like a resentful teenager than an equal partner, it was clear to us both that we had no future. I lamented the loss, but checked that fantasy off my list and settled into the ongoing project of mending my broken life. I was in my early thirties, mostly single, a little bit lonely, and every nerve ending tingled with possibility.

Jenny Bird also had two daughters, and we raised our children together. Her Jessie was the same age as my Jenny. The two girls were intertwined, like a vanilla and chocolate swirl ice cream cone. There was a well-worn path through the sagebrush between our houses, along which our children effortlessly flowed. They built fairy circles in the summer and snow castles in the winter. Both girls were ambivalent about clothing and often showed up in nothing but a pair red cowboy boots. I reveled in the ordinariness of my life as a mother to my daughters and a member of the flawed and beautiful family of humanity.

The one spiritual attachment I could not seem to give up was my devotion to Neem Karoli Baba—known as Maharaj-ji—the great sage whom Ram Dass had revealed in the pages of Be Here Now. Maharaj-ji was just iconoclastic enough to slip past my conditioned skepticism and override my newly cultivated cynicism. Maharaj-ji, too, was suspicious of religiosity. He had the gift of slicing through illusion with a single glance. He did not pontificate; he radiated. He was not pious: he was a rascal. And most compelling of all, Maharaj-ji was not even in his body anymore, and yet he continued to infuse and inform every aspect of my life. He was more accessible than any human being I knew. I had kept his picture with me since I was fourteen years old, and the combination of affection and mischief in his eyes had been the campfire in my wilderness. I took refuge there.

The scene that had unfolded around him was another matter. The only Neem Karoli Baba ashram outside of India happened to be right in my home town, and it was populated by a cast of irascible characters, endowed with many versions of genius, but seemingly unable (or unwilling) to function in mainstream society. Because I loved devotional chanting, I could not resist slipping over to the ashram now and then to sing to God (who I no longer believed in). I brought Jenny with me, and she would fall asleep in my lap in the temple room during kirtan, the call-and-response singing designed to invoke the divine attributes of the Hindu pantheon: the exiled lovers, Ram and Sita; Kali and Durga, the ferocious and tender faces of the Divine Mother; Shiva, Lord of Transformation; Krishna, God of Love.

At the heart of the Maharaj-ji's Taos ashram was a giant marble statue of the monkey god, Hanuman, which Ram Dass had commissioned a few years after his guru's death and shipped to America in the early 1980s. Hanuman is the quintessence of selfless service and devotion. He is also a trickster: playful and powerful, tender and undomesticated. Many of Maharaj-ji's followers saw their guru as an avatar of Hanuman, and they had built a Hanuman temple in his honor so that there was a place in the West where they could gather to remember the man who reminded them of the god, who reminded them to become the embodiment of loving service (God knows, they tried).

In the Hindu legend of the Ramayana, Prince Rama and his beloved wife, Sita, are exiled to the forest. Sita is abducted by the evil demon, Ravana, who carries her off to the island of Lanka, where he holds her prisoner. Hanuman rescues Sita (who represents the feminine aspect of the godhead) and returns her to Rama (the masculine aspect), thereby restoring wholeness to the cosmos. It is precisely because Hanuman thinks he is only a monkey that he is worthy of worship as a deity. This singular humility always appealed to me about Hanuman. I felt like just a monkey, too. Even when I had a sleazy pseudo-Sufi (a.k.a., Randy Sanders) trying to turn me into the Goddess.

•

I did not notice him right away. Like a leaf moth blending into the foliage, Jeff had spent a lifetime disappearing into his surroundings. I was vaguely aware that he was the father of several satsang children— including Kali, one of the little girls Jenny played with every week at the ashram—but I never heard him speak, nor was I inclined to engage him in conversation. I didn't interact much with anyone, actually. I went to the Hanuman temple to sing.

One day I ran into my friend Satrupa at the chai stand. She handed me a cup of hot black tea with milk, sugar, ginger, and cardamom and then poured one for herself.

"How's your love life?" she asked.

"I'm kind of with someone. He's a screenwriter." Michael Three claimed to have been Timothy Leary's personal assistant in the early seventies. He lived in Santa Fe, and though he seemed to wake up early every morning and write until the sun went down, at which time he commenced to drink late into the night, I never saw him actually produce anything. He also did not believe in monogamy, and I never knew when I drove the seventy miles to visit him whether he would be in bed with another woman when I arrived.

"Kind of with someone?"

"Well, you know."

"No, I don't."

I shrugged. "Me either."

"Because I know someone who's interested in you."

A cocktail of adrenaline and dread washed through my bloodstream. "Who?"

"Jeff."

"Who?"

"Him." Satrupa pointed across the outdoor dining area to the playground, where my love interest was trying to keep his teenaged daughter from wrestling the car keys out of his hand. They were laughing. Suddenly he spun around and tossed the keys to his middle daughter, who ran up the slide and then threw them back to her father.

"Too old."

"What? He's forty-eight. How old are you?"

"Thirty-six."

"That's perfect. What are you talking about?"

Here's what I was talking about: after squandering my youth on Randy Sanders, I was determined that my next life partner would be no more than five years older than me, preferably childless and dying to step right into a ready-made family. Jeff was a tall, middle-aged white guy with a receding hairline and three daughters, at least one of which was old enough to drive. Besides, he seemed too nice, too quiet. No edge. Boring.

"Nah."

Satrupa shook her head and smiled sadly. "Your loss," she said. "He's one of the best human beings I know."

•

The seed Satrupa planted managed to niggle its way into my psyche, and soon a small green shoot had sprouted. I kept thinking about Jeff, wondering if I was making a mistake to reject someone who appeared to be stable and warm, caring and witty. A grownup. And someone who wouldn't require an explanation about my devotional nature and my peculiar spiritual background.

I kept running into him around town. There he would be, opening doors for me at the post office or the bank, his eyes lingering on mine for a moment as I dashed past. He was leaning against the wall with his latte at the coffee house, watching me read my poetry on stage. He took all the children swimming in the Rio Grande on a summer day—including mine—and dropped Jenny off at home in the middle of a thunderstorm, running up to the porch holding my daughter's hand and then disappearing back into the rain. I made a point of ignoring him. Now that I knew he was attracted to me, I didn't want to give him the wrong idea.

And then there was Jonathan. After three Michaels, I still hadn't quite worked Jonathan out of my heart. Meanwhile, Jonathan had moved on without, it seemed, a backward glance. He lived nearby in Santa Fe, and I would see him now and then at satsang gatherings, which stirred the embers of illusion and blew smoke in my eyes, conjuring longings and regrets that kept me awake for a few nights before I came to my senses again. Jonathan had tidily concluded that the karmic purpose of our unrequited love affair was for me to break free of my monstrous marriage, and he was satisfied with his role as catalyst in my escape. Now five years had passed since our first kiss, it was late summer, and Jonathan was getting married to someone else. And he invited Jenny to be one of the flower girls at his wedding.

I blasted Melissa Etheridge on the car stereo ("Dance Without Sleeping") as I drove up the mountain road to the communal land where the festivities were to take place. I intermittently wept and muttered. Jenny sat beside me, casting nervous glances in my direction. She seemed to get that I was working things out. By the time we passed the raspberry ranch and began the last climb to the location of my beloved's wedding to another, I was determined to bless him on his way.

But my heart had not quite caught up with my mind. I released Jenny into the hands of the bridal party and headed to a small pagoda built on the edge of the meadow, opened the double doors, and entered. The space was profoundly quiet. I approached the altar at the end and bowed before a statue of the seated Buddha. Then I picked up a round black zafu and sat. I cannot do this on my own, I whispered, to no one in particular. You're going to have to help me. I opened my hands. Take it from me. Take this pain. After a few deep, slow breaths, I dropped into the stillness and rested there. I watched with awe as my old broken-heart story fell away like a sand cliff melting back into the sea. Then I stood up, walked out into the meadow, and bore witness as Jonathan married his tall blonde bride. And it was fine. It was totally fine.

After the ceremony, Jenny hooked up with the other temple kids and ran off to play, and I went in search of water. It was a hot day in late August—the same day as the anniversary of my wedding to Randy Sanders, as a matter of fact. I tried to put that association out of mind—both for my own sake and Jonathan's. As I approached the giant cooler where the drinks were kept, I saw Jeff talking with another wedding guest. So he does speak, I thought.

"Hi," I said.

Jeff looked around in an exaggerated manner, pretending that he could not believe I was actually condescending to address him. He pointed to his own chest, lifted his eyebrows, and mouthed the words, "Who me?"

I giggled like a girl, then blushed, then condemned myself for my flirty reaction. "Yes you."

"Hi." Jeff's smile was the smile of someone who had long ago learned not to take the world or himself too seriously. "Can I get you something?" His eyes were seawater green, his lashes dark and long, his eyebrows crazy, like Einstein's. I had never noticed how voluptuous his lips were, how perfect his teeth. His shoulders were broad, his torso long, his hips narrow. "Cerveza?"

I must have wrinkled my nose. "Of course not," Jeff said. "Beer. Yuck. How about a bottle of water?"

I nodded, and he opened the cooler. He handed me my drink, grabbed a Negro Modelo for himself, and sat down on the ice chest, gesturing for me to sit beside him.

"So I built your house," Jeff said.

"What?"

"You know the plans Tomas drew up for you?"

Tomas was our mutual friend, a fellow Maharaj-ji devotee who happened to be a contractor. When my father died, I had inherited fifteen thousand dollars—all that remained from the once robust estate left to him by his mother following her death less than a year earlier. Most my grandparents' money had been atomized by a combination of healthcare costs and what Dad called "the Jewish Mafia." I used my share to buy a piece of land on the Hondo Mesa, overlooking the valley where I grew up. I could just make out the roofline of my father's old adobe from the edge of my property. I wanted to build something, and in order to get a construction loan, I needed blueprints. Tomas helped me design a simple three-bedroom, one-bath, passive solar house. The bank rejected me three times. I was a single mother cobbling together a handful of part-time jobs—not a great prospect for managing a mortgage.

When Jeff approached Tomas about building a house on a piece of property he had recently purchased in town, he described what he wanted: a modest structure, a couple of small downstairs bedrooms and a larger one upstairs, one bathroom, big south-facing windows.

"That sounds just like what Mirabai designed," Tomas had said. "You know Mirabai?"

And so it came to pass that my secret admirer stole my blueprints and built my house.

Jeff finished his confession and said, "Would you like to come see it?"

●

A couple of days later, I drove up to Jeff's (my) house on a quiet street on the outskirts of town. When I knocked on the door, he answered with a dustpan in his hand. He was sweeping the floor. Something about this simple, homey act made me feel as if I had found shelter under a tall tree in a snowstorm. He invited me in.

"Sorry, " he said. "I didn't realize what time it was. I'm glad you're here. Can I make you a tea?"

"Please."

It was the most delicious cup of tea I had ever tasted. What was so special? A Bigelow English Breakfast tea bag, dunked in mug of hot water, mixed with spoonful of raw sugar and a splash of milk. I had brewed a hundred cups just like it. But Jeff's tea infused every cell in my body, warming what was cold in me, moistening what had run dry.

Oh Mirabai, I admonished myself, get a grip.

"So you're a stonemason?"

"Something like that." Jeff laughed. "Except much less glamorous. I install electronic locking systems in hotels."

"Those card thingies?"

"Yup. Those card thingies. So I'm on the road a lot. Like fifty percent of the time. When I'm home, my kids are with me." I watched him watching for my reaction to this revelation that his children are at the center of his life. I liked it, and I nodded. "How about you? You're a poet."

"Much less glamorous," I said, and he laughed. "I teach philosophy and world religions classes at UNM-Taos, and I run an office in my house making reservations for my family's eco-resort in Mexico."

"Resort?"

"It's just a small place—twelve cottages on a lake in the jungle. People bring groups—workshops, yoga retreats, family reunions. I make all the arrangements. I'm terrible at it. I can't even balance my own checkbook."

Having established how uninteresting and inept we both were, Jeff and I settled into a comfortable conversation. It turned out that Jeff had been with Joya in New York during the same time that I was there with Randy Sanders, only I (not surprisingly) didn't remember having seen him there. He had gone on to live for several years at Joya's ashram in Florida, where his first daughter was born. Jeff was a Vietnam vet. When he returned from the war, he had made a pilgrimage to India and had lived in spiritual communities on and off ever since.

He told me how the night before he was deployed at nineteen, he'd had in which he was shown that he would spend his tour of duty on the beach. Having grown up in Southern California, Jeff had been obsessed with surfing all his life and was more at home in the water than on land. He ended up being positioned as a lifeguard at a beach in Chu Lai where soldiers came to recover from the horrors of the front.

He told me about living with his teacher, Swami Rudrananda, "Rudy," in an ashram in New York City in the early seventies, and how Rudy would throw bolts of shakti across the room, sending people into orbits of ecstasy. Unlike Randy Sanders, Jeff did not seem to be inclined to romanticize the spiritual path. He tempered his dramatic accounts with just the right amount of irony and without a trace of arrogance. Plus his syntax was idiosyncratic and unexpected (it turned out that Jeff was dyslexic), and his voice was warm and rich, like his tea.

"You want to go hiking with me up in the ski valley tomorrow?" Jeff asked. "I'm leaving on a job the next day. I'll be gone for a couple of weeks."

"Tomorrow's Jenny's birthday."

"Won't she be at school?"

"Well, yeah, but . . ."

"So you can drop her off, take a walk with me, and get back in time to pick her up."

Work could wait. No one would perish if I couldn't confirm their reservation for another twenty-four hours. Besides, I worked for my mom. She would understand. Mom always understood. I had concluded that she basically just gave me money and pretended it was a job. I struggled not to take advantage of this arrangement, but there were always a thousand distractions. Kids to schlep, car breaking down. Friends in crisis, crises of my own. Dentist appointments and grocery shopping. At least this was something special. It always made my mother happy when I did something special for myself.

Jenny turned ten the next day. I dropped her off at school, covering her face with kisses before the other kids could see, and promised to come back with cupcakes at the end of the day. Then I drove over to Jeff's.

We never made it up to the mountains.

We ended up on his couch, listening to Tom Petty, Jimmy Cliff, and East Indian ragas.

"Can I kiss you?"

No one had ever asked me this before. It seemed so old fashioned, so cordial, so startling, I could not resist. I yielded to those squishy lips—like twin loaves of bread dough rising on a warm windowsill. I yielded to Jeff's ordinariness, which turned out not to be ordinary at all. Jeff was the kindest, most sensual, most interesting creature I had ever met. It was torture to peel my body from his when it was time to go pick up my birthday girl.

•

I did not particularly like the way Jeff's house turned out, but I liked him. A year later, it became our house, and I have lived there ever since.

"If you build it, she will come," Jeff would say, after telling our love story to dinner guests.

Which made me feel like a treasure, yes, but also exquisitely ordinary. A common woman, like billions of others, making a life with real man, in an imperfect house, with two interesting children—my youngest daughter, Jenny, and Jeff's youngest daughter, Kali—curled up together in one or the other of their beds downstairs. Our kids liked to believe that they had woven a web of magic so that their parents would fall in love and they could become sisters. And for a long time we all felt as if we were living in a fairy tale. Happily. Forever after.

CHAPTER 13

Radical Unknowingness

From the moment I first encountered San Juan de la Cruz (Saint John of the Cross) in Sevilla (Seville) during a semester abroad my junior year in college, I was infatuated. With his voluptuous love language, dripping with images of gardens and fires, secret wine cellars and hopeless intoxication, John struck me as the Rumi of Spain. Long before translators like Robert Bly and Coleman Barks had gotten their hands on the medieval Persian poet and rendered him so accessible that he had become the most popular poet in America, I had been reading Rumi as a Sufi master, rather than a literary figure. Now I had discovered his Spanish brother, and I followed them both into the wilderness of longing and took refuge with them beside the hearth of the Beloved.

Twenty years later, I was teaching John's mystical masterpiece, Dark Night of the Soul, in my college humanities classes, and my students were unimpressed.

"How could they not love this book?" I complained to my friend Sean.

"Maybe because it's exceedingly stuffy and pious?" Sean smiled.

"That's just the translation," I said. "In the original it's so juicy it's almost erotic."

"Then why don't you translate it yourself?"

"Me?"

"You could marry your three loves," Sean said. "That particular text, your fluency in Spanish, and your taste for beautiful language." Sean had watched me write two incomplete novels and a series of personal essays, casting about to find my own voice.

"I'll think about it," I said.

•

What happened to him? What lit the lining of Saint John of the Cross's heart on fire and sent the sparks flying across the centuries to ignite countless other hearts (like mine)?

Nothing special, as it turns out. Just another version of the human condition. The ordinary suffering of what the Buddhists call samsara: life on the wheel of births and deaths, rolling toward liberation.

Here's what we know: He wasn't born Saint John of the Cross; his birth name was Juan de Yepes y Alvarez. He was born in 1542, only fifty years after the Great Expulsion, when the Catholic Church banished Jews and Muslims from their homeland, where they had not only managed to live in relative harmony under Islamic rule for almost eight centuries, but also collaborated on the some of the greatest and most enduring works of art, architecture, mathematics, science, and esoteric mystical teachings in human history. The atmosphere of sixteenth-century Spain was still permeated with the fragrance of this convivencia—the intermingling of Abrahamic faiths that characterized the so-called Golden Age of the Andalusia. (We might rightfully suspect that things weren't always golden between the children of Abraham, but it was a notable step in the direction of reconciliation and mutual respect.)

As one of many children to a single mom, John almost starved to death in his early life, and severe malnutrition stunted his growth. He barely reached five feet (just like me!), and his luminous black eyes dominated his face. His father—probably an aristocratic Catholic with secret Jewish roots—died when John was a baby, and his mother—probably a beautiful and marginalized dark-skinned Moor—wandered from village to village with her children—half of whom perished—selling the yarn she spun by hand. When he was a teenager, John found work in a hospital where, with the tenderness of a mother soothing an infant with a cold, he tended outcasts who were dying of syphilis. His empathy and intelligence caught the attention of the hospital administrator, who sent him to Salamanca and paid for his education there. The university of Salamanca was the center of learning throughout Europe and the Middle East at the time, and it was there that the young mystic was probably exposed to the teachings of the Sufis. Hence the not-so-coincidental-after-all resemblance between his poetry and Rumi's.

John was intense. He hunted for God like a wolf in winter. He pounced on monastic life in the hope that it would transport him to the heights he longed for, but discovered instead that the Church was mired in rules and regulations that had nothing much to do with the power of the Gospel teachings he loved and evoked little more than a mediocre piety that depressed him. Shortly after his ordination as a Carmelite friar at age twenty-five, John decided to bail on the whole ecclesiastical enterprise and head up to the mountains to live as a holy hermit like the desert fathers and mothers of third-century Palestine.

Teresa of Avila—radical reformer, institutional troublemaker, and passionate mystic—heard about this fiery little monk who had lost all patience with organized religion and wanted only to sit quietly with God. She summoned John to meet with her at her newly established convent for "Discalced" (Barefoot) Carmelites, named for the hand-woven hemp sandals the sisters wore as a symbol of voluntary simplicity.

"I understand," the middle-aged nun said to the young priest after he had unburdened his heart. "And I agree with you. The Church has lost her way, and things are a mess. You can either wave goodbye and go off and tend your own soul, or you can join me and help change it."

He bored into her eyes with the dark fire of his eyes. She did not flinch.

"Alright," he said at last. "As long as it happens soon. I don't have any time to waste."

Teresa laughed and clapped her hands. "You are the true companion of my soul."

•

Once the two mystics joined their flames, the blaze galloped through the mainstream Carmelite order, sweeping some members into a joyful embrace and pissing off others. When John was twenty-nine, a band of Carmelite thugs snatched him from his bed in the middle of the night and imprisoned him in a monastery in Toledo. They locked him in an airless cell that had previously served as a latrine. The space was so small he could not stretch out his diminutive frame when he lay down to sleep. The monks let him out once a day and took turns flogging him while the others ate their midday meal and watched. John was fed on minimal scraps and, never robust to begin with, grew frail, his back and legs striped with oozing welts that would not heal. For nine months he had no covering but the single robe he was wearing when he was arrested. In the sweltering heat of summer this woolen garment rotted off his body, and in the winter he shivered with cold.

Meanwhile, the brothers would congregate outside the door to his cell and gossip in stage whispers. John had been forgotten, they murmured; no one cared about him. Teresa's movement had been crushed, and there was nothing left to defend. Still John refused to renounce the reform. But little by little his faith began to darken. His faith in Madre Teresa and her vision for a contemplative life. His faith in a God who seemed to be entirely disinterested, if he existed at all.

Two things saved John's sanity: poetry and the night sky. There was a single window high above him, and he tracked the constellations as they drifted across the tiny square of air. John was an amateur astronomer, famous for grabbing young monks from the chapel and taking them on spontaneous stargazing expeditions in the hills and fields around the monastery. "See this?" he would say, sweeping his hand across the firmament. "This is where you will remember who you are, and catch a glimpse of the One who made you."

In captivity, deprived of writing materials, John began to compose poems in his head and repeat them until he had memorized them. Then he would recite them back to himself, like lullabies, and find comfort there. One day a sympathetic guard overheard the sublime poetry flowing from John's closet. The next morning, when the monks were at Lauds, the guard slipped a scroll of parchment and a quill into the prisoner's cell with his bowl of rice.

It seems likely that the same kindly man who helped the patron saint of poetry meet his destiny also helped him escape from prison. One night John managed to climb the high wall of his cell, crawl through the window, and, using a rope made of knotted sheets, let himself down the steep façade of the monastery. Then he crept across the courtyard, scaled the wall, and followed a black dog through the darkened city streets to one of Teresa's reformed convents, where the nuns enfolded him and nursed him back to health.

One day, as John sat recovering in the convent garden, his most famous poem poured from him like an overflowing bucket of rain: On a dark night / inflamed by love longing / O, exquisite risk! / Undetected, I slipped away / my house, at last, grown still . . . That sweet night: a secret / Nobody saw me / I did not see a thing / No other light, no other guide / than the one burning in my heart . . .

It was eight stanzas of distilled sensuality, in which the narrator (an apparently feminine figure) speaks of climbing "a secret ladder in disguise" and making her way through impenetrable darkness to a lush and radiant sanctuary where her Beloved waits. She lays down on his "blossoming breast," and he (inexplicably) reaches up "with his gentle hand" to wound her neck. Suddenly all her "senses are suspended." She flies up out of herself and is gone.

Shyly, John read his masterpiece to the nuns before Vespers that evening. "So what do you think?"

They must have blinked at him in astonishment. Had their esteemed priest lost his balance in prison and turned to composing erotic literature? If it hadn't been for the precedent set by Solomon's juicy love poem, Song of Songs, John's piece would have been a scandal. As it is, the nuns were anxious to protect their mentor from further persecution.

"Father?" The abbess knelt at his feet. "Maybe you could write an exposition, explaining each stanza and showing us how this poem is a guide for our own . . . spiritual journeys."

"Good idea, Sister."

And so Dark Night of the Soul—one of the most incandescent

jewels of the religious canon in any language—was born.

*

People walk around all the time claiming that they're having a "dark night of the soul." His lover loves someone else. Her cat was diagnosed with leukemia. He blew out his ACL in a skiing accident. Her best friend from childhood overdosed on heroin. Maybe all these things happened to a single person within a short time period—a year, say— which makes the sufferer feel entitled to call his cluster of troubles by such a grandiose name. Sometimes we watch other people navigating life's unanticipated (yet not uncommon) obstacles and we sympathize: "Poor thing," we say. "She's been going through a dark night of the soul."

Maybe. But probably not.

What she's going through is a really rough time, and it might make her grow and galvanize and appreciate life more. But this is not what John of the Cross was talking about when he coined that term five hundred years ago.

What John was referring to was an intensely personal—often invis- ible—spiritual crisis, which actually turns out to be a great blessing. It may at first mimic a state of existential angst, when life drops its dis- guise and religious beliefs seem inadequate to address the nakedness, but it is also infused with a quality of yearning, a quiet resonance with the deepest chords of the human condition. It is a gift that can only be given when we get out of our own way. This ability to surrender is in itself an artifact of the kind of spiritual maturity very few of us ever reach. This doesn't mean we "earn" our dark nights through our own efforts. What it means is that we have allowed our cup to be shattered, and that the Holy One may (or may not) come along and refill it with light. It means that we have said yes to annihilation, without any expectation that we will be resurrected.

See if this sounds familiar:

You have been on a spiritual path for a while now. You have devel- oped a yoga practice, attended meditation retreats, cultivated centering prayer. You read sacred texts and self-help books and the poetry of the mystics. You chant kirtan or Taize or sing in the church choir, assist the priest at the altar or fast on Yom Kippur. These practices have reliably opened your heart and made your spirit soar. They have connected you to a felt experience of the sacred, and these holy moments have hooked you and gotten you through the times that weren't quite as juicy. Everywhere you turn you see evidence of these higher realities. You are bombarded with magical coincidences: a favorite friend calls just when you are thinking of him; you dream of your long-gone grandmother, and she tells you exactly how to handle a troubling relationship with your teenager; a flock of wild geese lifts off from a snowy field, and you glimpse the perfect order of the cosmos in the pattern of their flight.

Then, gradually or all at once, all these ripe spiritual fruits dry up and turn to dust. You cannot meditate your way through the emptiness. Chanting starts to sound silly in your mouth. You find the holy books to be almost unbearably pedantic. What once filled your heart now leaves you cold.

There must be something wrong with you.

Or so you conclude. Erroneously.

What's happening here, says John of the Cross, is that you are becoming an adept. This is good news! The Holy One sees that you have grown and that She can begin to wean you from the Divine Breast. It's time for Her to put you down and set you on your wobbly feet. She is offering you "the crusty bread of the robust." And what is your response? To throw a spiritual tantrum. John says that this is exactly like the time the matriarch and patriarch, Sarah and Abraham, threw a big party to celebrate the weaning of Isaac. The adults were having a great time eating figs and drinking wine, but baby Isaac sat in a corner and wailed.

This is understandable, John assures us. We are hungry for what we have grown out of. Like the Israelites crossing the desert, who woke up every morning to a feast of manna covering the ground (which, John points out, contains the exact flavor each traveler loves best), we push away the divine food and demand the "meats and onions" we ate in bondage back in Egypt. But we can no longer access that connectedness to the sacred we had come to expect. This is the first part of the dark night of our souls: the falling away of attachment to the way the inner life is supposed to feel.

And if this "Night of the Sense" was not harrowing enough, a certain intellectual emptiness creeps in and takes over. Now you can no longer even conceive of the Divine in any kind of a meaningful way. All the conceptual constructs you had erected as scaffolding to climb up to God—using materials you had inherited from your parents, perhaps, or scavenged from the religious organizations you joined in your youth—begin to crumble. The whole spiritual thing makes no sense anymore. This is the advanced version of the dark night of our souls, "the Night of Spirit," when our attachment to any ideas we have had about God dries up and falls away.

The best thing to do when the unraveling begins to happen, says John, is . . . nothing. This may seem counterintuitive. We think if we pray harder and sing louder and fast longer, we will get the spiritual high back. God's plan will be revealed, and the universe will make sense again. But our efforts to rectify our brokenness only make it hurt more. What we need to do is drop down into the arms of the darkness, surrender to feeling nothing and knowing nothing. Then, John promises, an "ineffable sweetness" will seep up into our souls from the Ground of Being and fill us with a peace we have never known.

Our only task is to stop trying so hard and simply be.

John uses this analogy to explain things: It's as if a great artist (the Greatest Artist Ever) were painting our portrait (because we are so beautiful and captivating), and we refuse to hold a pose. We keep moving and changing positions. "How's this, God?" we say, cocking our head at a fetching angle. "Don't you prefer my profile?" We would be disturbing the master, John says, preventing him from completing his masterpiece! Sit down and shut up, John says. (Well, he doesn't exactly say that, but this is my "translation" of what he says. I'm a translator.)

Here's the other paradoxical and utterly wonderful thing about the dark night of the soul: it's not really dark at all; it's dazzlingly bright.

The trouble is, we have not yet developed the inner eyes with which to behold such radiance. And so it blasts our perceptual apparatus, and we experience the divine light as darkness. Like Plato's prisoners fettered all their lives in an underground cave, watching shadow plays on the wall and taking this for reality, when we finally break our chains and climb up and out into the real world, we are blinded by the light of the sun. It takes a while for our eyes to adjust. We must be patient with ourselves, John says. We must be willing to hang out in the darkness for as long as it takes to see the light.

And so, as you can see, the way people generally refer to the dark nights of their souls has very little to do with the state of spiritual maturity John of the Cross was speaking of. It's a misnomer to suggest that our ugly divorces and intimate losses—the ordinary components of life in human form--qualify as true dark night experiences.

Or is it?

When I began writing my translation of Dark Night of the Soul, I was a bit self-righteous and judgmental about this lack of understanding of the original meaning of the term, and also compassionate and determined to gently set people straight on the matter. By the time my book was published, I had a very different interpretation of these teachings. Tragedy and trauma are not guarantees for a transformational spiritual experience, true, but they are opportunities. They are invitations to sit in the fire and allow it to transfigure us. Who, you might ask, would sit in fire? Who would be crazy enough to do that?

CHAPTER 14

The Little-Starrs

The summer I signed the contract for the new translation of Dark Night, my mother and my boyfriend teamed up to help me meet my deadline. Mom released me from the reservations desk for the family eco-resort in Mexico and hired a real person to take my place, but she still gave me my monthly paycheck. Jeff overcame his anxiety about blending our families and invited Jenny and me to move in with him and Kali so that I wouldn't have to pay rent while I was working on the book.

My first task was to sit with everything I thought I knew about the Dark Night of the Soul and allow for the possibility that I did not really understand this text at all. That willingness to know nothing, as it turned out, was the very essence of the teaching.

My own radical unknowingness had only just begun.

•

Jeff made a point of having alone time with Kali and encouraged me to do things with just Jenny. Jeff would take Kali skiing or out for blue corn pancakes at the Taos Inn. Jenny and I would hike down to the confluence of the Rio Hondo and the Rio Grande and, sitting on a blanket on the sandy river bank, she would fill me in the books she was reading, the thoughts she was thinking, the emotions she was feeling.

Although happily bonded with Kali, I could tell that Jenny did not yet trust Jeff, and she still pined for the years when I was a single mom and she was my only child—her big sister off mothering children of her own. Jenny circled Jeff like a coyote checking out a human, and he responded by giving her space. Too much space, I thought. I wanted him to scoop her up and be the father she never had, but he wanted to let Jenny connect in her own way, at her own pace.

When we all came together at the end of the day, I felt like a bee finally finding its flower. I perched on the lip of the blossom and drank. I prepared homey little meals of spaghetti and turkey meatballs, green chile stew and corn muffins, or fried tofu and veggies, and we ate together as a family. We watched videos or helped our kids decorate poster boards for school projects. Jeff and I tucked our children in, woke them up, packed their lunches, dropped them off, picked them up, and—for the first time in my life—I was at home in the world.

Every morning after the kids had left for school, I lit a candle at my desk in the bedroom I shared with Jeff and settled down with my copy of Dark Night of the Soul in its original language, a massive English-Spanish dictionary, and the only two extant English translations of the text (one by a professor named Edgar Allison Peers and the other by a priest named Kieran Kavanaugh), which I used for reference when I got stuck. I had never met anyone who had actually gotten through either English version of this book. Most people found the existing translations stilted and scholarly and, well, too religious.

Page by page, I washed off the dust of the centuries so that John's perennial wisdom could shine on the rest of us. While the teachings sent shivers of soul-recognition up my spine and the poetic language made me swoon, the project soon shifted from a literary exercise to an inner cataclysm. The outside of my life was a sun-drenched orchard. Inside, a quiet darkness was inexplicably dropping.

Everything I had always wanted was coming true, and I was bereft. I felt like someone I loved had died, or was dying. Maybe it will be me, I thought. Maybe this work is my swan song, and when it's finished, my life will be over.

●

Jenny started her period. That helped to explain her recent unbridled brattiness, which had been darkening her world from horizon to horizon, leaving me feeling unaccountably guilty. Our hormones must have been insidiously mingling in the molecules of the air.

"What is your problem, Dude?" I exploded one afternoon when everything that came out of my mouth was met with her disdain.

"C'mere," Jenny said, and I followed her into her room and sat beside her on the bed.

When she told me she had started bleeding at school, I squealed and laughed and hugged her. I launched into a speech celebrating her entry into womanhood and praising the holiness of this moment in her life. I threatened her with a ceremony to be held in Jenny Bird's kiva on the mesa. She groaned.

When Daniela had started her period nine years before, I took her out into Miranda Canyon with a newly menstruating friend of hers and her friend's mom. The four of us built a small fire and sat around it. The mothers gave special power objects to the daughters and offered prayers. I cannot remember the gifts now. Hardbound journals with batik covers, maybe, and special pens. Gourmet chocolates and woven friendship bracelets. We probably prayed that our daughters would become strong and happy women who loved themselves enough to be of service in this troubled world.

Jenny took her rite of passage into her own hands. It was a Saturday, and Jenny rode her bike over to the Hanuman temple. I didn't question her motive. Our girls often spent weekends there, weeding the garden, watching younger children on the playground, scrubbing pots and pans or baking cookies for prasad (the food offered to the guru and then fed to the people as a blessing). We were happy that they wanted to hang out at the ashram drinking chai instead of scoring drugs at the park.

Jon, the temple manager and a former hair stylist, seated Jenny in a chair on the lawn. Spontaneously, a small crowd began to gather around. Jenny was famous for the luxurious chestnut curls that cascaded below her waist. With reverence, Jon lifted Jenny's long locks and snipped them, then followed with the buzz of the electric razor. People gasped, laughed, and finally cheered. Then, in a moment of iconoclastic instinct, Jon went into the temple and emerged with a small vial of sandalwood oil reserved especially for the Hanuman murti, with which he proceeded to anoint my daughter's head.

When she rode into the driveway at sunset, I looked up from my computer and out the bedroom window. My heart thrummed in my chest. The seven seconds it took me to bound down the stairs and throw open the front door gave me the time I needed to collect my wits and greet her with the respect she deserved.

"You look beautiful, Honey."

She handed me a plastic bag stuffed with her tresses. "Can we send this to Locks of Love, Mom?" Jenny said. "I want some kid with cancer to have my hair."

And we did.

I would have liked to direct Jenny's coming-of-age ceremony myself—or at least share in it—but all I could do was bow to her innate wisdom and dignity.

•

There seemed to be another aspect to Jenny's decision to shave her head. For most of her life, Jenny had lived in a nest inhabited by just the two of us. Daniela had left home when Jenny was only seven. My lovers had come and gone, and my mom and sister were always there for reinforcement, but the foundation of our household was consistently Jenny and me. Our stuff. My money. Solitary decisions. Though she had expressed a yearning for a whole family, I could see that Jenny had the impulse to assert herself within this matrix as independent, unpredictable, bold.

Yet I also saw how much she still loved to be tucked in at night. To have her big bald head covered in kisses, just as I used to part her long tresses to kiss her ears. She still begged me to ease her into sleep with "the cloud"—a guided meditation I had used with her since she was small—inviting her to visualize herself climbing onto a fluffy white cloud in a clear blue sky and riding it like a magic carpet over mountains and pastures and beaches. I knew she still wanted to be woken in the morning by a mommy who climbed onto her bed and swung her own dripping hair in her daughter's face to rouse her. How she appreciated being ordered to call by five p.m. when out riding bikes with friends. How deeply my new young woman-child still needed me.

CHAPTER 15

Invisible Child

It was late July in the Sangre de Cristo Mountains. We had borrowed a canoe from Jeff's partner, Johnno, strapped it to the roof of Jeff's truck and headed to Heron Lake a couple of hours to the northwest. We drove along the shore as far as we could until the road was no longer passable, and then Jeff, Jenny, Kali, and I packed the vessel with our gear, hoisted it above our heads and traipsed through the marshes to a remote campsite Jeff had scoped out among a grove of willows. We set up our tents, and Jeff took the girls for a swim while I set up the kitchen and started dinner: bean-and-cheese burritos and salad.

The frying pan was too small for the tortillas, and I'd forgotten to bring butter. I shredded my knuckles on the cheese grater and dropped the cheddar in the dirt. The sound of my family squealing in the snow-melt did not warm my cockles; it raised my hackles. Here I was in paradise with the people I loved most, and everything was vexing me. By the time they emerged from the lake, dripping muddy waters all over my neatly organized cooking area, I had fully fledged into a bitch. I managed to criticize Jenny's manners, wardrobe, and attitude over the course of five minutes, which provoked her silent fume and set our most intractable patterns into high gear. The deeper she sulked, the more agitated and demanding I became. I couldn't stop myself. Finally Jenny stomped away, and I crumpled in tears.

"I don't know what's wrong with me," I admitted when my daughter and I went for a walk after dinner to make peace and reconnect. We were holding hands.

Jenny stopped, took my other hand in hers, and beamed at me.

"Maybe you're pregnant," she said.

"Ha!"

All those times in my twenties when I longed to be released from the non-procreation agreement I had forged with the universe, I remained steadfast and stubborn. In my thirties, once I finally allowed myself to consider the possibility of pregnancy, the universe snubbed me. Now I was almost forty, living with the person who had quietly revealed himself as the true love of my life, and I had let the whole pregnancy fantasy go.

Besides, when I been with Michael Two and had started taking birth control pills, my body had reacted to the invasion of fake hormones by building up a mass of uterine fibroids, which (according the results of an ultrasound) had rendered the wall of my womb virtually impenetrable to sperm. I didn't even think about pregnancy anymore.

That night I writhed in my sleeping bag beside my lover. My fibroids were killing me. Whenever I turned over it felt like I was rolling on top of a sack of rocks embedded in my pelvis. That's it, I decided. I'm having a hysterectomy. It's time to get this thing out of me. I had tried every alternative remedy on the planet: acupuncture, herbs, diet, shamanic cleanses, and chakra balancing. The fibroids only seemed to be growing.

I made an appointment as soon as we returned home. A pregnancy test is standard procedure at the gynecologist's office, and so upon arriving I peed in a cup and placed it behind the sliding door between the bathroom and the lab. Then I was marshaled into an examining room where I waited for over an hour, trying to distract myself by analyzing People's choices for the sexiest man alive.

When the nurse came in at last, she was clearly in a rush. Busy day at the women's clinic. She tossed the dark blue strip onto the counter beside me. "It's positive," she said. "Go ahead and get undressed from the waist down, and the doctor will be in shortly."

"Positive?" My world tilted on its axis and almost toppled. I had a couple of college degrees, but suddenly I couldn't remember what positive meant, in the medical sense. When you tested positive for the AIDS virus, for instance, did that mean you had the disease? Shouldn't it be negative, because your whole world was about to go up in flames? Wasn't this bad news that I was pregnant and had a womb that had no room to grow a person? Or by "positive" did she mean that I should be happy I wasn't actually pregnant and could get on with my plan to shed my diseased uterus once and for all?

"You're pregnant," she snapped, one centimeter away from adding, "you idiot!"

"That's not possible," I said. "I'm infertile." It was ludicrous to argue with this busy person who was fully capable of telling the difference between positive and negative pregnancy results, but I couldn't integrate the information. It felt like an immaculate conception, only they got the wrong girl.

"The doctor will be in shortly," she repeated and left the room.

Dr. Heidi and I discussed my options. She explained that if I were to try and carry this baby, I would need to do so under the supervision of a high-risk pregnancy specialist, that I would have to spend the next eight months in bed, and that they would stockpile my blood in the likely event of a late-term miscarriage, which would endanger my life. Given my age and the ravaged condition of my uterus, she recommended terminating the pregnancy.

"An abortion?"

She nodded benevolently, although whether it was from compassion for my loss or pity for my lack of the most basic biological facts I could not tell.

When I broke the news to Jeff, there was not much to discuss. He didn't want to take any chances of my dying in childbirth, and I didn't want to make him start all over raising a child when he had worked so hard for so many years to support the three he had. He held me while I cried, and told me that if only things had been different he would have loved to have a baby with me. Brave and resolute, we scheduled the abortion and planned to follow up with a hysterectomy as soon as I was recovered enough to undergo the surgery.

There were only a couple of clinics in the state willing to "terminate pregnancies," and they had waiting lists. So I had to spend two weeks incubating an embryo that would never become a child. I reckoned

I had two choices. I could either distance myself from my condition until I could get it over with, or I could show up for the experience of carrying life inside my body for the first and last time. I opted to be as fully present to reality as I could manage. I called my friend Bobbi, who had been our family therapist before she retired, and she agreed to come over and help me come to grips with my impending loss.

"Have you picked out a name?"

"Bobbi!" Had she forgotten why I had asked her here? "I'm not having the baby."

"I know, but I think you need to make a relationship with this unborn being. It didn't come into your life for nothing." We were sitting side by side on my couch. "Talk to it. Tell it that you would have been thrilled to be its mommy, but that it isn't going to work out this time around. Send it on its way with love. You'll feel much better if you do."

I closed my eyes and reached out to the little soul hovering nearby. "Mo," I said, opening my eyes to look at Bobbi. "I'll call him Mo. After my father's favorite uncle." Mo. Short for Moishe, Yiddish for Moses, the baby whose mother sent him in basket of reeds down the Nile to escape persecution. Moses, who God called from within a bush that burned and was not consumed, who took off his sandals because he was standing on holy ground. Moses, who received the Torah at the summit of Mount Sinai and led his people right to the edge of the Promised Land. But I was not thinking of the Bible when I named my unborn son. I was thinking of the legendary Uncle Mo. I was thinking of my father, who died before he had the chance to meet the father of my doomed baby. I was thinking five girls were enough and that we needed a boy, even if he would never become a real boy.

Bobbi placed her hand on my cheek, and I came undone. I collapsed against her, and she stroked my hair. From the dark cavern of Bobbi's lap, I spoke to little Mo and tried to make things right. Bobbi was correct: it helped. Guilt gave way to a kind of holy wonderment. I spent the next two weeks nauseous and exhausted, in awe of the miracle of life growing inside me, aware that it was fleeting, which made me cherish it all the more.

•

Jeff was working out of town the day of the procedure, and so my mother accompanied me to the clinic in Santa Fe. The night before, she wrote a kind of love letter about my pregnancy and my choice to end it. She wrote with reverence and poetry, lifting the tragedy into the realm of the sublime without in any way minimizing my pain. She expressed gratitude that I had the opportunity to create new life with a man I love. She affirmed the importance of a woman's right to choose what happens to her own body, and praised the doctors and nurses who take care of us when we conceive a child and elect not to bring it into this world. Jeff, a former yogi who did not believe in petitionary prayer and had long ago dismissed the notion of a personified deity, promised he would be silently chanting Sri Ram Jai Ram Jai Jai Ram throughout the day as he stripped old key locks from hotel room doors.

Before the procedure I met with a counselor who gave me one more chance to change my mind. I did not waver. Then I had a blood test and an ultrasound to determine just how pregnant I was. More than I thought. When I glanced up at the screen, I saw a distinct black spot, about the size and shape of a kidney bean.

"Is that the baby?" I asked.

"That is the embryo, yes," the technician told me.

"It looks . . . fine," I said.

"Yes," she agreed.

Someone led me into the operating room where someone else inserted a giant needle into my uterus, injected me with a local anesthetic, and left me alone to stare at the ceiling for a half an hour.

"My little bean," I murmured. "My sweet little Mo."

I granted myself permission to cry, but the numbness spreading through my loins seemed to have migrated to my heart. I felt nothing. I floated on the surf of my breath until the doctor came in and vacuumed little Mo from my womb.

•

The following June I underwent what they call a partial hysterectomy. There was nothing partial about it. My uterus was severed from the fallopian tubes that fastened it inside me, and then it was pried through a slit at bikini line. They did leave my cervix and ovaries in tact, so presumably my body would still follow the twenty-eight day ovulation cycle, following the moon like a tide that ebbed but never flowed. I would not bleed. I was expected to be relieved about this. Yet I found myself mourning my period. I missed the earthy smell of the menstrual blood, the aching in my loins and the oozing between my legs as the walls that lined my uterus melted and shed, carried away each month like a Tibetan sand painting. A continuous rotation of crucifixion and resurrection enacted on the cross of my own body, devoid of tragedy or drama.

In less than a year I had terminated the only pregnancy I would ever experience and then forfeited any possibility of becoming pregnant again. I sat with these facts as my body slowly healed around the void to which I had been compelled to assent.

CHAPTER 16

Slipping

My daughter was losing her mind.

It wasn't easy to spot her unraveling; Jenny had always been eccentric. As a child she would burst into storms of delight when we encountered twin baby boys in a double stroller at the park, or discovered that the peach seed she planted in an old teacup has sprouted a tiny peach tree, or realized that the human body is comprised of eighty percent water. After I had finished reading aloud from Bless Me, Ultima or The Lion, The Witch and the Wardrobe, my eight-year-old would exclaim, "I love adjectives!" Jenny was enthusiastic about random things and defiantly indifferent to what others held in esteem.

Jenny's adolescence seemed more tumultuous than most. I mean, I knew, from having been a teenage girl myself, that puberty could be brutal. And I didn't think it was possible to raise a more difficult daughter than Daniela, who was totally shut down when she was with me and totally out of control when she wasn't. But Jenny had been perfecting her passive-aggressive attitude and seemed to relish every opportunity to let me know what an uncool fool I was. She seethed with quiet rage and built a wall between us that I could not seem to scale. When I did manage to clamor up and peek over the rim, she beat me back down. I felt like Sisyphus. I kept rolling my rock back up the hill.

When Jenny started ninth grade, she received a full scholarship to Chamisa Mesa, the alternative high school I had founded with Randy Sanders ten years earlier. When I left Randy Sanders, I took a leave of absence from the school, and my colleagues there had flowed into the space I left behind so that there was no room for me to return. The University of New Mexico had opened a branch campus in Taos around the same time, so I applied for a position to teach philosophy and religious studies, and that was that. I graduated from being a high school teacher to being a college professor. Randy Sanders had left Chamisa Mesa a few months later and then left town forever. Soon it was as if we had never existed. The school flourished, and now my baby girl was going there.

Among a circle of bright, iconoclastic, wildly creative teenagers, Jenny's own radiance intensified. Always concerned for the well being of Mother Earth, she quickly became an environmental activist. Temperamentally inclined toward anarchy, she turned into a human-rights activist, too. Drawn toward altered states of consciousness, she embraced the role of a pot smoker. Where Jenny had spent her preadolescence hiding behind shapeless flannel shirts and baseball caps, now she was wearing tight camisoles and coloring her hair bright purple. Overnight, it seemed, my daughter had a new tribe, a new identity, and I was, by definition, an outsider, not to be trusted.

She excelled in school, as she always had. And she still spent a lot of time at the Hanuman temple, where she had begun to cook for the large crowds of starving hippies that gathered on Sundays for a free meal. So I tried not to worry. But when she began to go to parties and not come home, I blamed her new school.

I called the office manager and expressed my concerns.

"You remember how it is at Chamisa Mesa, Mirabai," she said. "These kids are like a family. They look after each other. And they adore Jenny. They will make sure she's safe." This made sense to me, and I relaxed.

Meanwhile, Jenny discovered string theory and Spalding Gray. She turned fourteen. Osama bin Laden blew up the twin towers and the Pentagon, and Jenny protested U.S. plans to invade Afghanistan. Although only a couple of months apart in age, Jenny had started high school, while Kali was still in eighth grade. These two girls, who had spent the past four years as a single intertwined being, began to drift apart. Every once in a while, my old Jenny would come back to me.

We would cook a meal together, or discuss the genocide of Native Americans, or hike up into the aspens, and the warmth of our love would thaw the hurt between us and all would be right with the world again. Same with Kali. They would hardly speak for days, and then Jenny would crawl into Kali's bed, and they'd whisper and giggle in the dark until they fell asleep curled together like a wave enfolding the shore. That's how powerful this child was. She could shut all the light out of a room with her gloom, or she could light up your heart and make you feel worthy and safe.

·

It was March. Jenny was playing loud music in her room. Well, actually it wasn't music; it was rap. It was mean and ugly. The noise throbbed through the wood door, oozed around the corner into the hallway, and infiltrated the kitchen where I was grading papers at the table. Kali was in her own room, drawing. Jeff was upstairs doing bookkeeping for his business.

Primed for a fight, I took Jenny's music as an act of aggression. I stalked over to her room and pounded on her door. "Jenny, please turn that down!"

No response.

"Jenny, turn down your music!"

She turned it up.

I don't remember what happened next. I ranted. Jeff charged down the stairs and banged on Jenny's door. "Jenny, listen to your mother and turn down the music!" He stomped back upstairs. This was the first time I had ever seen Jeff angry. I didn't know whether to be grateful that he had come to my defense or worried that he might have hurt my daughter's feelings.

Jenny's door flew open. She rushed into the kitchen, grabbed a knife from the drawer, pushed past me back into her room, and locked the door. "I'm going to kill myself!" she shrieked.

I threw myself against the door. "Jenny, open up!" No response. I watched myself become hysterical.

"Jeff!" He came back down. "She has a knife."

I ran outside and around the house to the door that led from Jenny's room to the patio. Her back door was open, and Jenny was gone.

An early spring storm had dumped a foot of snow and the ground was covered in a frozen blanket, which draped over the sagebrush and glimmered in the light of a waxing moon. I rushed through the yard, crying her name. Jeff walked beside me, calling more gently.

Silence. Footprints in the snow. Moon shadows.

I called the police.

•

When Jenny first came to me, she used to slip into catatonic states. If something threatened her—a new person to meet, someone criticizing her performance or behavior—Jenny's eyes would glaze over, her mouth would grow slack, and she would not move or make a sound. After many unskillful attempts to reach her, I learned to hold a quiet space for these episodes and not try to snap her out of it. I figured some invisible scab had been accidentally torn from an old wound and she needed to bleed in peace. I would be waiting on the other side.

Although the state police station was only a few blocks away from our house, the officers on duty the night Jenny threatened suicide could not find us. Jenny wandered back home on her own about an hour later. She was catatonic. I hadn't seen her like that since she was a small child. Her bare feet were rigid from walking through the snow. Kali burst out of her room and tried to rush into Jenny's arms, but Jenny's arms hung limp at her sides. I guided my daughter over to the couch and gathered her against my body.

Kali took the down comforter from her own bed and wrapped it around Jenny. She sat on the other side of the couch, pulled Jenny's frozen feet into her lap and held them. Jeff made tea and wedged the cup into Jenny's hand, then gently lifted it to her lips. I rocked her, cooed to her, whispered and wept.

The next morning, Jenny behaved as if nothing unusual had occurred the night before. She wasn't pretending. The spot where

Jenny had scared us to death by threatening suicide seemed to have been covered over by an opaque film in Jenny's mind. I saw no reason to peel it off, and we moved on.

                                   ●

One morning I met Jenny at the Taos Diner, where she had been dropped off after a party up in the mountains. I had expected her to be home by 11:00 the night before, but she had called to tell me all the kids had been invited to sleep over so they wouldn't be driving under the influence of drugs or alcohol. I grappled with anger at being duped into letting her party all night and relief that she was trying to be responsible about it.

As I walked into the diner, I decided to use my father's technique. Instead of judging the morality of my daughter's life choices—which would only make her defensive—I would simply and authentically inquire about her life, in hopes that she might open up. "So what's in your head these days, Cookie?" Daddy would ask me when I called from some ashram in New York or a cabin in the redwoods. It validated my sense that my own experience mattered, and made me feel grown up and interesting.

My little girl was sitting alone at a booth, pouring sugar into a cup of coffee. When did she turn into a caffeine fiend?

"Hi, Honey."

"Hi, Mom." Her eyes were wary.

I slid in beside her and hugged her.

"So, Jenny."

"Yeah?"

"I realize that you've been on a journey, and I'm wondering: what kinds of things are you discovering?"

I knew it sounded hokey, but it worked. Jenny's eyes widened with surprise and pleasure, and her words tumbled out. She told me about talking all night with a boy about the Heisenberg Uncertainty Principle and how we could not perceive reality without impacting it with our observations. Their conversation had led deeper and deeper into the wilderness of abstract thought and opened at last into the realm of spirit, where all things took their rightful place and then dissolved into undifferentiated being. At that point, Jenny had experienced a merging with Ultimate Consciousness, and now this was all she wanted.

"I feel like I understand everything, and I don't need to be here anymore."

"What do mean?" I tried not to sound shrill. "Like, you could die?"

Jenny nodded. "But don't worry, Mom. Not yet. My work here isn't done."

•

Jeff had a contract to install locks at a resort hotel on Waikiki Beach in Oahu. He suggested that we use this as an opportunity to pull the girls out of school and take a family vacation in Hawaii. We figured that after a week, I would take the kids back home to the mainland, and Jeff would head to Kauai for his next gig.

In the late sixties, Jeff had briefly gone AWOL when he was home on leave from Vietnam and hopped a stand-by flight to Honolulu to go surfing. Now, four decades later, he wanted to find the place where he had camped out in an abandoned chicken coop on the North Shore, and take our daughters bodysurfing in his favorite surf spots. We loaded up the boogie boards and headed across the island.

My fearless daughter, as it turned out, was terrified of the waves. She clung to Jeff's hand as they sloshed beyond the shore break, and he swam her out to where the water was calm and they could catch the waves and ride them in on their bellies. Not a strong swimmer myself, I watched from the beach, grateful that my fatherless child had a loving man to share the mystery of the ocean with her. When it was Kali's turn to bodysurf with her dad, Jenny and I waded out to a sandbar and stood side by side in the shallow water, watching yellow-striped angelfish and luminous blue parrotfish swim around our toes. Whenever they brushed against our calves, Jenny squealed and clung to me.

It reminded me of when Jenny was younger and we flew to the

Yucatan every year to stay with my mom, who spent her winters on Laguna Bacalar, along the Belize border. We always started or ended our trip with a few days in Puerto Morelos, visiting our friend Fernando. A former physician, now free-spirited massage therapist, and fellow devotee of Neem Karoli Baba, Fernando was one of the few adults Jenny not only tolerated, but appreciated. He took her swimming in remote cenotes in the jungle, made banana smoothies and homemade almond milk, bought fairy wings for Jenny and a pair for himself, and then wore them as they strolled the streets of his village.

Fernando took us snorkeling. We paddled out to the barrier reef, tied our kayaks to posts, and slipped into the shallow water. Jenny was afraid of the manta rays that sometimes flapped their wings beside our shallow boat as we dipped and pulled the oars. She would grow rigid whenever she spotted one—or even imagine that she had caught a glimpse.

But as soon as we squeezed into our fins, strapped on our masks, inserted our snorkels and pressed our faces to the water, all Jenny's anxiety would dissolve in wonder as we entered this underwater universe we had. Holding hands, we would float over the surface of the reef among schools of tropical fish, which darted into the crevices of the coral forest and exploded into view.

•

The sweetness of our day at the beach in Hawaii was temporary. Back in the car, we were fried by the sun and famished, and it didn't take long for a fight to erupt between Jenny and me. Our triggers had become finely tuned over the past year or so. Throughout her childhood, Jenny had been compliant and loving, as if she feared I would change my mind and give her back if she misbehaved. She saved all her mischief to dump on Jenny Bird and Greg, the parents of her best friend, Jessie, whenever she spent the night at their place. Now, she seemed to disdain me in proportion to the degree to which she had formerly worshipped me, and I was not handling it gracefully. I had enrolled us in parenting classes. I knew I was the adult and she was the adolescent, and it was my job to hold reasonable boundaries while remaining calm and compassionate—blah, blah, blah—but I was incapable of stopping myself from reacting when she pulled the exactly perfect maneuver designed to provoke me. It seemed to amuse Jenny when she got me to flip out. I felt more like a trained circus animal than a skilled parent.

There was one morning a few weeks before we went to Hawaii, when I was folding laundry on the bed I shared with Jeff, and I was overcome by despair. Jenny and I had had a particularly challenging morning, and I wasn't sure I would be able to survive her teens. I suddenly thought of Randy Sanders and how he had stolen my youth and saddled me with these difficult children. If only he hadn't hijacked my sexuality, preventing me from having a normal relationship with a regular guy. If only he had been willing to accommodate my desire for a baby once it became clear to me that Armageddon was not immanent and I realized I really did want to have babies. If only I had had a real husband who I could fuck and fight with and question and desire. If only I could have had children in whose eyes I could see my own reflection, and the reflection of my father, and my grandmother.

The resentment that boiled up in my belly was ferocious. I doubled over with its force. But a small part of me witnessed this flood of emotion with calm curiosity. Welcome to the human condition, my witness whispered. This is just another chapter in another life. Not so special. And in that moment my victimhood lost its integrity and melted away. I returned to the task of matching up my daughter's socks.

On the way back to Waikiki from the North Shore that day, Jeff, Jenny, Kali, and I stopped in a Thai restaurant for an early dinner. Jenny had been radiating hostility throughout the meal, but, like her sister Daniela, she had perfected her offensive tactics to such an extent that the shots she fired were invisible, which made my response look even more ridiculous. While we were waiting for our check, I finally snapped, and Jenny and I had one of the worst fights of our life, while Jeff and Kali looked on in helpless horror. At one point, Jenny said, with icy calm, "Why don't you give me up? I know you wish you had never adopted me."

She was right. Sort of. There had been one small moment when I did consider giving Jenny back. She had only been with us for a few months when I left Randy Sanders, and her adoption was not yet finalized. He had convinced Daniela to live with him. Having been with a much older man for more than half my life, and finding myself mothering a child old enough to be my sister, I was poised to experience autonomy for the first time. It was not too late to change my mind about adopting Jenny by myself. I could have my life back. I confessed these thoughts to my mom and Ramón, who assured me they would support me in whatever choice I made, but also encouraged me to keep my beautiful little girl, with whom I had already fallen in love. So I shook off the illusion of freedom and renewed my vow to be Jenny's mother. No matter how difficult our relationship sometimes was, I never again doubted my decision, and Jenny never knew of my heart's secret betrayal. Or at least I thought she didn't.

Now, for the fist time, Jenny was expressing doubt about my unconditional commitment to her. I scrambled to assure her that I loved her, that I wanted her, that she was the most important person in my life, but I was still furious, and I said all this through clenched teeth. Jenny smirked and rolled her eyes. We drove back to the condo in silence.

As we entered the resort compound, I asked Jeff to pull over and let me out. "I need some time alone," I said. I shut the door without saying goodbye. Jeff and the kids drove on to the hotel, and I headed for the beach—as I had often walked up into the Talpa foothills when Jenny had pushed me to the verge of the hysterical zone—and tried to calm down. A half moon spilled onto the sand and glittered off the whitecaps. Body moving through space, feet connected to the earth, my sanity was gradually restored. I returned to the condo, determined not to lose my temper ever again—or at least not on this trip.

When I walked in, Jenny was gone. She had slipped out when Jeff and Kali were putting away the groceries we had picked up from a produce stand on our way home. We launched a search, looking for her everywhere—in the fancy lobbies and beachside snack bars, in the hotel disco. Defeated, we returned to the condo to call security. When we walked in, Jenny was sitting on the couch watching TV. I leapt across the room and pulled my daughter into my arms.

"Don't you ever fucking do that to me again!" I sobbed, covering her face with kisses. "I was so worried. I thought you had run away."

"Nah. I just needed to be alone for a while," she said, mimicking my declaration of a couple of hours earlier.

"Ha ha."

Jenny surrendered to my embrace, and we cuddled on the couch, channel surfing. Jeff slipped away to tuck Kali into bed, and peace dropped its sweet blanket back over our little family.

That was the second time in a year I thought I had lost my daughter.

●

The third time came just a couple of days later—our last full day in Hawaii. We drove over to the Hanauma Bay Nature Preserve, and this time Jenny sat in the shallow water among the tropical fish with a radiant smile as they darted under her knees and nestled in the cups of her hands. On the way back to the condo, we stopped off at another favorite beach from Jeff's youth, to take a final dip in the Mother Pacific. This time Jenny dove into the waves with Kali and sailed back to shore as if she had been bodysurfing all her life. Jeff, proud surfer papa, looked on.

Suddenly a huge wave gathered behind Jenny. She stood up and turned her back on it, and the wave crashed over her. Jenny was gone. She tumbled in the surf for what seemed like a very long time, her purple curls occasionally bobbing to the surface and then disappearing again. I screamed.

"It's okay," Jeff said. "It will be over in a minute, and she'll be fine."

I raced to the shore to meet my bedraggled child as she rose on her hands and knees, sputtering. Her cheek was scraped and so were the palms of both hands and one knee. I draped her arm over my shoulder, and we limped back to the car. Jenny was quiet, stunned, humbled by her encounter with the wild face of the sea.

Later that day, I caught sight of Jenny on the balcony of the condo, her arms propped on the railing, gazing out at the ocean. Her lips were moving rapidly, and her eyes flashed with enthusiasm. I peered closer to see who she was talking to. Was Kali sitting beyond my view? No, Jenny was alone. She was carrying on an animated conversation with herself.

I walked into the bedroom Jenny shared with Kali, and Kali was sitting on her bed reading. "What's up with Jenny?" I said.

"What do you mean?"

"She's outside talking to herself."

Kali giggled.

Later, Jenny confronted me. "Kali told me you think I'm crazy."

I blushed. "What do you mean?"

"She said you thought you saw me talking to myself, and now you think I'm nuts."

"No, I was just joking."

"Okay."

"But . . . are you?"

"Insane?" Jenny grinned. "That's for you to decide, Mom."

•

On the last morning of our Hawaii vacation, Jeff suggested that he take Kali out for breakfast and I take Jenny. He thought it would be a good idea if we each had some one-on-one time with our daughters after having been together all day, every day, for a week. Jenny chose a little Japanese café we had been passing on our walks down to the beach, where she was attracted to the photographs they posted in the window of unidentifiable platters of seafood and rice.

As we were descending in the elevator, I touched a scatter of red splotches on Jenny's neck. "Wow, Honey, you really got bruised when you got knocked over in the ocean yesterday. I hadn't noticed that before."

Jenny shrugged away from me, looked down at the floor, then back into my face.

"Yeah, I guess."

"Well, I called the chiropractor and scheduled you for an adjustment next week when we're home."

"K."

We walked to the restaurant in companionable silence and ordered. As we were waiting for the food to come, Jenny said, "Mom, there's something I need to tell you."

"Uh-oh."

"Please don't be mad."

"I can't promise that, but I can promise that I will listen and try to act like a grown-up."

"Well, me and Kali kind of snuck out last night."

"Kind of snuck out?"

"Mom! You promised."

"Okay, go on."

"We went down to the beach and met up with some guys." My heart was hammering, but I kept quiet. "They were Hawaiians. They walked with us, and we sat down and talked, and they were really cool."

"What else did you do with these cool Hawaiian guys?"

"Kali didn't do anything with hers. I kissed mine." She bit her lip and glanced at me. Then she touched the red marks on her neck. "These are hickies."

I laughed. I wanted to reprimand her for lying to us and interrogate her about the actual extent to which she had ventured into sexual territory, but she seemed so innocent and bewildered and, well, happy.

"Was it fun?" I asked.

"Oh, Mom, it was amazing! It was like meditation, but much better. When you're kissing someone you are . . . like . . . totally present."

"Yeah, it is like that." I squeezed my daughter's hand, and we ate our Japanese breakfast. My intuition told me she had not gone any further than kissing, though I couldn't be certain. I decided I would give it space for now, and let Jenny bask in the sweetness of her first kiss.

CHAPTER 17

Divine Mother?

On the first day of summer vacation between second and third grade, Jenny broke both her arms when she hit a bump and sailed over the handlebars while riding bikes with her friends. I called my friend Jim, an orthopedic surgeon, who met us at the emergency room, where he took over Jenny's care. Within a couple of hours, Jenny had two casts—one purple and the other pink—and we were back home with pain pills and mango sorbet. Jenny and I sat on the couch and came to grips with the fact that for much of her vacation Jenny would be incapacitated, and that I would have to do almost everything for her.

Jenny curled up in a tight ball on the couch and closed her eyes. I sat beside her and watched while her brow, furrowed in consternation, begin to relax. Soon she was breathing deeply. When she woke up a couple of hours later, the sun was beginning to set, washing the living room with that ethereal New Mexico light. Jenny asked me to put Bob Marley on the stereo, and she stood up slowly and unfurled her bright, broken arms like wings and began to dance. She dipped and turned, stamped and swayed, and a smile splashed across her face and flooded her body. She danced through three songs, and I danced the last two with her. Then she sat down on the couch again, panting, and gave me a decisive nod.

Every little thing was going to be all right.

•

It was the last day of Navaratri, a nine-night festival in honor of the

Divine Mother. For the past twenty years or so, devotees would gather at the Hanuman temple every evening at sunset to sing to the Goddess and offer incense, firelight from butter lamps, and garlands of marigolds. On the final day, Durga Puja, prepubescent satsang girls were dressed as kumaris (representations of the goddess Durga as a child) and seated beside the sacred fire as one older girl knelt before each little one and offered an assortment of delicacies from a round metal plate: fingerfuls of buttered rice, green grapes, miniature Reese's Peanut Butter Cups. Now that Jenny had started her period, she had taken her place as an elder, who served the Goddess by serving her miniature representatives.

After the kumaris had been satisfied, devotees loaded up a van with a consecrated statue of Durga that had been fashioned just for this occasion, packed a basket with little lights made of ghee, gathered drums and bells, and headed north out of town to the confluence of the Rio Grande and the Rio Hondo. On the riverbank, the goddess was placed on a small raft woven of red willows and tied with wild grasses, surrounded by tea lights, and sent off downstream, carried by a tide of chanting and drumming. As the sun sank behind the canyon walls, washing the river in golden light, we watched her float away.

•

Our flight from Hawaii landed on the morning of Durga Puja. We had missed most of Navaratri, and Jenny and Kali were eager to get over to the temple the moment we got home from the airport so that they could participate in the final ceremony. I was exhausted, having slept only intermittently during our two connecting flights to Albuquerque, followed driving by three hours to Taos. I needed a nap. So did Jenny, who confessed to not having slept during the entire flight. But, in spite of my plea that they stay awake to keep me awake, the girls had both conked out in the back seat and slept through the entire drive from the airport.

When we finally pulled up to the house, the girls reluctantly agreed to give me an hour's rest, and I stumbled upstairs to bed. Jenny set the alarm on her digital watch and woke me precisely sixty minutes later so that I could drive them to the temple. In a daze, I dropped them at the gate and headed back home to unpack. Kali hadn't seen her mother in weeks, so the plan was that we would all meet up at the river at sunset, and after the closing ceremony, Kali would go and spend the night with her mom, and Jenny would come home with me.

I hiked down the trail and arrived at the riverbank just as Durga was being prepared for her journey and pushed gently into the current to the sounds of bells and drums and shouts of "Jai Ma!" and "Ki jai!" I found called out to Jenny, who was congregating with her friends and doing her best to pretend we weren't related. Irritated and still tired, I was ready to leave as soon as the last drumbeat had been sounded and the goddess had disappeared in her little boat around a bend in the river.

"Let's go, Jen."

"Mom, can I stay at the temple tonight?"

"Honey, we just had a long trip. I want you to get a good night's sleep."

"I will get a good night's sleep."

"In your own bed."

Jenny fixed me with her most ferocious gaze, and I caved.

After ten years as a single mom, I had learned to pick my battles with my daughter. A speedy analysis of this situation came up in Jenny's favor. It was only Saturday. I had planned our return trip from Hawaii so the kids would have the weekend to recover before the new school week started. Tomorrow, after the morning chanting at the temple, Jenny could come back home and get settled.

"Let me check in with the caretakers. If it's okay with them, it's okay with me."

It was fine with the caretakers. They loved Jenny. But I left feeling disempowered and vaguely guilty, as if I had allowed myself to be bamboozled into turning in an exam for which I was neither prepared nor qualified.

●

The next morning, as I was getting dressed to go over to the temple to chant chaleesas, the phone rang. It was Stephen, a caretaker at the ashram.

"Mirabai?" His voice was hesitant.

"Yes? Is everything alright?"

"Um . . . "

Adrenaline shot up the crown of my head. "Stephen, did something happen to Jenny?"

"She's acting strange."

"Strange?"

"Yeah. She was wandering around the grounds almost all night. People kept waking up and finding her out in the garden." He paused. "Naked. Except for a prayer shawl."

"What was she doing?"

"Singing."

I took this in.

"We covered her and brought her back to bed. Three times. But she was up at dawn, and she went right into the temple room. She's been there ever since. Now she's dancing in front of Baba's tucket." Stephen attempted a chuckle. "At least she's dressed," he added.

"I'll be right there. Don't let her leave."

"We'll try. But it's Sunday. We're getting ready for a hundred guests."

"I know, I know. I'm sorry." I had always dreaded being perceived as a pain in the ass. "Thank you, Stephen."

As I drove over to the ashram, I tried to figure out what might be making my cool daughter act like a nut. A combination of sleep deprivation from our all-night flight and participation in a potent religious rite must have dislodged Jenny's inhibitions. I just needed to get her home. A quiet evening with a bowl of green chile chicken soup and an episode of The Hitchhiker's Guide to the Galaxy on video should calm her down. Me too. I suddenly craved normalcy with a ferocity that took me by surprise, as if the footings of my world were melting and only something quintessentially ordinary would prevent its complete and irrevocable disintegration.

When I walked into the sunroom that led to the temple, Jenny was sitting at a table with her head in her arms. Kali was perched on a bench, sketching her. I placed my hand on my daughter's back, and she raised her head in slow motion. She looked at me with unfocused eyes, and very gradually, she smiled.

The radiance of Jenny's smile almost blinded me. Gone was the grumpy adolescent. In her place was a beatific goddess-girl who beamed at me with unconditional love.

"Hi, Mom."

"Hi, Sweetie." I hugged her. She laid her head on my shoulder and clung to me. "What's going on, Buddy?" She did not answer. She did not loosen her grip around my neck. I turned toward Kali and lifted my eyebrows.

Kali shrugged. "She's been this way since I got here. She hasn't said a word. Except just now, when she said hi to you." Kali returned her attention to placing the finishing touches on the drawing of her apparently God-intoxicated stepsister.

•

We were sitting on my bed, sipping Earl Grey. After a long nap, Jenny had begun to come back to herself, though there was still a thrumming silence around her that made me feel like I had entered an empty church in a rainstorm.

"Mom?"

"Yes, my love?"

"Can I go to the peyote meeting at Lama tonight?"

I almost choked on my tea. "Are you kidding me, Jenny? Look at you. You want to alter your altered state?"

"I wouldn't take any peyote. I won't even go into the tepee. Jack invited me to be his assistant." Jack was the fireman, whose sacred task it was to tend the campfire through the night while the participants in the ceremony prayed and sang inside the dark womb of the tepee, occasionally stumbling outside to throw up in the sagebrush as they metabolized the magic in their mushrooms.

"I'm sorry, Jenny. You're too . . . you're not . . . Let's try this again in the spring, okay?"

Jenny did not say anything, so (as usual) I felt compelled to say more. To say too much. I launched into a lecture about the power of these ancient medicines and how they needed to be approached with utmost respect and not as recreational substances, and Jenny stared at me while I pontificated. I watched her watching my mouth move, then shifting her gaze to my eyes and perceiving something there, but not actually listening to my discourse.

Suddenly Jenny wriggled her fingers in the air between us—a cross between "The Itsy Bitsy Spider" and the Jesus blessing—and said, "It's all just a game of pretend."

"What?"

She looked up, down, and all around, to indicate the full spectrum of phenomenal reality.

I commenced a fresh sermon. This time I preached about how I, too, understood that the world was ultimately an illusion, but that I was a big fan of this place nonetheless, and that I, for one, had learned to embrace the mind as a vehicle for transcending the mind. This, I explained, was the path of Jnana Yoga.

Jenny continued to gaze at me with a kind of affectionate pity, and I stopped talking. We sipped our tea.

Then I said, "I'm sorry I have to say no sometimes, Honey. I'm just trying to be a good mom."

Jenny reached for my hands and pressed them between hers.

"I know," she said. "You are a good mom. You always have been."

These are pretty much the last coherent words she ever said to me.

●

It is not always easy to spot when someone you love is losing her mind. Several conditions obscured Jenny's mental illness at first. One was that Jenny prided herself on her unconventional attitudes anyway, so it seemed at first as if she might simply be producing and starring in her own existential drama. In many ways, Jenny was a typical teenager, and I had rationalized her behavior over the past year (and everyone assured me this was so) as being nothing more than an extreme version of adolescent angst—a pain in the ass, but developmentally appropriate.

Also, when Jenny's psychosis switched on, it manifested (as it does with many mad geniuses) as a spiritual experience, and the holiness she radiated was undeniable. She was beatific. Anyone who came near her was bathed in light. It was a couple of days before I was able to reconcile the fact that my daughter was experiencing a psychotic break and a mystical state. They were not mutually exclusive. I should know. After years of trying to figure out what the hell was going on with my own altered states, which had begun at the same age as Jenny was experiencing hers, I had pretty much concluded that I had been suffering from a severe case of dissociation. Evidently I had developed this slipping away action as a coping mechanism for my untenable circumstances. But I was also (as Randy Sanders—I hated to admit this—suspected) experiencing a profound and authentic glimpse of the numinous.

Jenny's adoption file had revealed that her birth mother suffered from severe bipolar disorder and had been hospitalized on and off for most of her life. Like Jenny, Gloria had a very high IQ. When she was not locked up, she made her living as an exotic dancer in Albuquerque's red light district, which is (a) how Jenny was conceived and (b) why Jenny was taken away at age two, when she was found alone in a motel room where she had been left for several days without food. But my understanding was that while there is a genetic predisposition for mental illness in the offspring of people with such chemical imbalances, the child might not inherit the disease, and if even if they do, the onset does not usually occur until the late teens. When I thought about it all, which was rare while I was immersed in the daily task of mothering Jenny, I figured we had a few more years before we needed to be looking for signs. So far, she hadn't been showing any. She was moody, yes, and judgmental as hell, but also a high achiever with a sophisticated sense of humor and a capacity for deep empathy.

●

Days after Jenny's last day on earth, as I was trying to piece things together in the futile attempt to make sense of the senseless, Jenny's friends told me what happened after I'd left her at the river the night of the Durga Puja.

They had hiked upriver to the hot springs, and as they soaked together under the rising moon, they passed around a joint. Jenny, a fledgling pothead, took a hit and handed it to the guy next to her. A few minutes later, she began to cry. This in itself was unusual. Jenny was not someone to cry easily, especially in front of people. But that night, once she started she could not stop. She wept, she sobbed, she howled. Her friends took turns holding her in their arms. A young woman named Rachel, who helped out around the Hanuman temple, told me later that it seemed like Jenny was feeling and releasing a lifetime of pain—maybe lifetimes. At last, Jenny rose silently from the spring, wrapped herself in a blanket, and went to sit by herself on the riverbank. Her friends concluded that she needed space, and they left her alone.

Like Jesus in the wilderness between his initiation by John the Baptist and his emergence as the Messiah, Jenny had grappled in private with forces I can only imagine. She had never returned to her ordinary consciousness after that.

●

The next few days following Durga Puja unfolded in a dreamscape of beauty and anguish. Jenny was too unstable to go back to school. I brought her home; she ran away. I made her a sandwich, and she created a peanut butter and jelly mandala in the middle of her bed. I reached for her, and she growled like a wounded dog and tried to bite my hand. Desperate, I took her to Kali's mother, a self-described shaman whom Jenny loved, to see if she could bring my daughter back from the other world she had escaped to. She tried, but Jenny had slipped beyond the reach of her powers.

Daniela had an early Monday morning appointment with the dentist for Jacob's first check-up, and she needed help with Bree, so I volunteered Jenny. Maybe being responsible for a two-year-old would ground my unhinged younger daughter. As a teenage mother (twice), Daniela had always needed a lot of help, and her kids spent as much time at our house as they did with Daniela and her various boyfriends. Jenny loved babies, and from the time she was eight years old, she had fed, diapered, and comforted her sister's children with competence and calm. Daniela and I decided Jenny would sleep over so they could just get up and go the next morning. But she was still acting odd. That night, Jacob woke to the sound of Jenny crying. He went to get his mom. Daniela came into the kids' room, where Jenny was lying on the top bunk.

"What's up, Babe?"

Silence.

"Jacob said you were crying." Daniela reached for her sister's hand in the dark. "Why are you crying, Hon?"

"Because it hurts."

"What hurts, Jenny?"

"Giving back."

"Giving what back?"

"Giving back to God."

•

On day three of Jenny's episode, I had an idea: I would buy her a trailer. We had been talking about it since summer. Our friend Adair, a social worker, had endorsed the plan. "It's called a Teen Cabin," she said. Teenagers need their own space, Adair explained, but they also need to stay safely held within their parents' sphere of influence. The solution, if you could pull it off, is to arrange for close but separate living quarters. That way, kids who are bursting with the juices of individuation can see what it feels like to be independent without being prematurely emancipated. I couldn't help but wonder, wistfully, why both my daughters had been so eager to get away from me, but I comforted myself with the thought that I too had left home young, and I adored my mom.

Our friend Trudy, who used to live in Taos, was visiting from California, and I heard that she had an Airstream for sale. I had just received the second advance check from my publisher, so I had money in my pocket. I would buy Jenny the RV, set it up in the yard, and Jenny could create her own world out there, coming in to eat and bathe and watch movies when she felt like it. I would even throw in a cat. I loved cats, but I was allergic, and Jenny had always wanted a kitty of her own.

I tracked Jenny down for the umpteenth time at the ashram. This was the only place she seemed to want to be. She would sit before Maharaj-ji's tucket, laying her face against the plaid blanket draped over a platform to represent his presence, her eyes closed, lips moving. Periodically she would rise up on her knees and begin fluttering her fingers in front of his picture, weaving the air with complex hand mudras. She would stand and whirl, sit and stare, bow and remain prostrate for a long, long time.

I clanged the bell over the temple door as I entered, but Jenny did not look up.

"Jen?" I touched her hair. She whipped her head toward me, eyes wild. I drew my hand back. "Let's go get your trailer. Trudy's meeting us at Elaine's."

In silence, Jenny rose to follow me.

"Sweetie? Shoes?"

She shook her head.

"It's October, Jenny. Almost November. You have to wear shoes. It's cold out."

Without a word, she whirled around and took off running. She leapt over the irrigation ditch and onto the adjoining property, where she darted between the back porch and the tool shed. When I finally caught up with my daughter, I blew up. "Jenny, this is bullshit!" She stopped in her tracks and stared at me. "I have to get these copyedits in by the end of the week, and I'm spending all my time chasing you around." Jenny surprised me with a look of compassion. "I'm a writer who's not writing," I said plaintively, more to myself than to her.

"I know, Mom." She spoke at last. She hugged me, and we walked back to the car.

"You drive," she said. "I'll walk."

"Jenny, Elaine's house is five miles away."

She ignored me and began walking.

I started the car and inched up beside her. I leaned over and opened the passenger door. "We can stop at the animal shelter on the way back, and you can pick out a kitten."

She climbed in.

But we did not make it to Elaine's to meet up with Trudy. As we were driving past the turn-off to Chamisa Mesa high school, Jenny opened the door to the car and tried to get out. I swerved to the side of the road, running over shards of broken glass and cursing.

"Jenny, are you crazy? You can't get out of a moving car!"

"I need to pay off some debts." As part of my effort to bribe her into going home with me the day before, I had given Jenny her allowance a week early. Now it was around 3:30, and school was just letting out for the day. Absently, I wondered who Jenny owed money to and why.

"What about the RV?"

She slammed the door. I rolled down the window.

"What about the cat?"

She shrugged.

"I want you home by 9:00!"

She nodded and trudged up the hill to the school.

●

I drove over to Elaine's in a fugue state.

When I walked in the door, Elaine and Trudy were sitting on Elaine's couch having tea.

"Jenny's losing it," I said from the doorway. "I don't know what to do." I stood for a moment, arms folded, clenched, and then I started to cry.

My friends set down their cups in unison and I went to them, melting into their collective embrace.

When I finished explaining how Jenny had been acting for the past couple of days, Trudy said, "This is a psychotic break, Mirabai. You need to take it seriously. People in this condition think they're invincible, and they walk in front of trains. You need to get help for Jenny. Right away."

"I'll make some calls and see if I can get her a bed in the adolescent unit," Elaine said. "I still have connections at St. Vincent's from when I was a psych nurse."

Psychotic break? Psych ward? We were hereby shifting into serious territory.

I nodded my head. There were those at the ashram who were lauding Jenny as an incarnation of the Divine Mother, but I had to face the fact that my illuminated daughter might be seriously ill. If a psychotherapist Zen teacher and a Sufi psych nurse were telling me Jenny was in danger, I had to do what I could to protect her, right? I had to. The seams of my daughter's mind were bursting, and something vital was spilling out. I was her mother. I would intercept the disaster. I would save my crazy, holy, beautiful girl.

CHAPTER 18

Dark Light

After I left Elaine's, I drove out to the Hondo Mesa, not knowing what had become of my wild child, or when I would ever find her again, or what I would do with her when I did. It had only been three days since Jenny had begun to act like a lunatic, but it felt like this drama had been going on forever and would never end. All I wanted to do was go home, but I was like a person who gets into an accident on her way to the bank, and as the paramedics are trying to staunch the bleeding, she keeps repeating, "I have to get this deposit in by 2:00."

I had promised Jenny Bird that I would come to the CD release party she was throwing for all the people involved in the project, and, under the influence of shock-logic, I was determined not to let my friend down.

The recording engineer was at the party with his fiancée.

"When's the wedding?" I asked.

"Valentine's Day."

"Que romántico." I sipped my cup of wine. "Planning to have children?"

The woman reached for her lover's hand and squeezed it. They looked meaningfully into each other's eyes, and then they both smiled at me. "Yes."

"Don't," I said. "It's not worth it."

I thought they'd laugh. But they didn't. They looked at each other again, this time nervously.

"Just kidding," I said and left the party.

My daughter had sort of promised to be home by 9:00. It's not that I expected her to uphold the agreement, but I needed to be there just in case.

Jenny was not home when I got there.

I called everyone I could think of who might know someone who might have some clue as to where she could be. I finally tracked her down to a one-room adobe shack up the road from our house. A boy Jenny went to school with, whom I had never met, was living there with a single mom in her thirties. After an hour of coaxing, he managed to get Jenny to climb into the open bed of his pickup, and then he transported her the one mile to our place. When he dropped her off, he was awkward and brief. He seemed embarrassed by the whole situation.

"I found her in my roommate's car," he said. "She was dismantling the rear-view mirror and stabbing the seat covers with a fork. I'm going to have to pay for that."

Jenny smiled hugely, hooked one arm onto a post that held up the porch, and began to twirl, the other arm flung behind her. The full moon washed the sagebrush with pewter light and illumined the planes of Jenny's face.

"I'll take care of it," I said. "Just let me know what it comes to. And thanks for bringing her back."

"Okay," he said and bolted.

Jenny crouched, as if she were about to spring and run away again.

"How about something to eat?" I said. "Cheese tortellini and pesto. Your favorite."

Her expression shifted from beatific to menacing in a flash. She growled, snarled, shot out her hand as if it were a claw. Involuntarily, I gasped and recoiled. Jenny chuckled and followed me inside.

As I boiled the water for pasta, Jenny climbed up on the couch and began to step daintily along the back. She proceeded to make the rounds of all the furniture in the house, circumambulating the edges like a cat. I tried to keep an eye on her as I cooked, but she disappeared into Kali's room.

I rinsed the tortellini, spooned it into a bowl, mixed in a dollop of pesto, stuck a fork in it and knocked on the bedroom door. Silence. When I entered, the room was dark, and it took a moment for the edges of Jenny's form to take shape in the shadows. She was crouching at the far corner of Kali's bed, eyes glittering. I handed her the dish of pasta, and she reached for it, then whacked it out of my hand. The hot food spilled across my arm, my shirt, the rug at my feet. Jenny shimmied past me and rushed out of the room.

I heard the front door open and then slam. It was very cold outside. Jenny was barefoot, and wore only a short, tight tank top with her favorite royal blue parachute pants. I left the food on the floor and went after her.

"Sweetie?" I sang into the darkness. My voice was shrill, fake. "Want to go see Kali and her mom? They invited you over," I lied.

When I had picked Jenny up the day before, Kali's mother had warned me against a psychiatric intervention, on the grounds that "they would turn her into a mental patient for the rest of her life."

Meanwhile, Elaine and Trudy were telling me that if I didn't get Jenny help immediately something terrible was likely to happen.

Torn between these two categorical opinions, I tried to quiet my mind and seek inner guidance. Nothing.

●

I ducked inside, grabbed my purse, and tried act casual as I dashed back outside and headed toward the car.

"Let's go, Honey." I had no idea where we would go once I got behind the wheel, but I was trying to buy time before Jenny ran away again. To my amazement, she followed me and opened the passenger door. Thank you, God, I uttered. I climbed in and began to babble, flinging words around in hopes of hitting on the right combination to regain her trust, pretending this was an ordinary jaunt to visit friends, rather than a desperate late-night flight into the void.

Jenny froze and stepped back.

"What? Oh, come on, Jenny. Just get in the car."

"Be quiet and listen," she whispered, holding a finger to her lips. "I've always tried to tell you. Be quiet. Listen."

"Okay, okay! I'll stop talking if you just come with me."

She put her hand on the door, hesitated, withdrew it, leaned over and stared me down through the glass across the span of the front seat.

I got out and walked around the car to open Jenny's door for her. She stepped aside and ambled into the sagebrush. Slowly, as if pursuing a wild partridge, I followed her. She could not cover much ground without shoes. I easily caught up with her, and I clasped her shoulder, turning her around and guiding her back to the car. I helped her in, closed the door, closed my eyes, and prayed. Then I walked around to my side of the car and got in.

Jenny got out.

I got out.

I crossed the driveway and reached for her hand. She let me lead her back to the car. I started the engine and drove to the top of the driveway, irrelevantly put on my blinkers, and turned left onto Maestas Road. As I accelerated, Jenny opened her door and tumbled out, then sprang to her feet and took off.

I screeched to a stop in the middle of the street, flung open my door, and, leaving the engine running, plunged into the darkness. She was gone. Defeated, I headed back to the car.

Suddenly Jenny materialized out of the shadows and slipped into the driver's seat. She slammed the door, gunned the engine and sped away.

I dropped to my knees in the empty street. "Oh no," I whispered. "Oh no."

＊

I walked back to the house and called Anthony, a former lover who had become a big brother. Anthony had fulfilled the bad-boy-on-a-bike archetype I'd needed as part of my recovery from Randy Sanders. He was brooding and sexy, with a fuck-you attitude toward the world that I hoped would rub off on me. It didn't. But once we had dispensed with the illusion of a romance, Anthony and I had been able to get on with the business of being friends. If I had a flat tire or my pipes froze or I locked myself out of my house, it was Anthony I would call.

Now that I was with Jeff, I had stopped depending on Anthony to rescue me, and we had begun to drift apart. But Jeff was still working in the South Pacific when my daughter went crazy and took off in my car, and so it was Anthony I summoned to do something—anything— to get her back.

While Anthony was at the state police office filing a report, I called my real boyfriend in Hawaii and told him what happened. I had been keeping Jeff apprised of Jenny's condition ever since Sunday morning when I found her channeling the Divine Mother over at the Hanuman temple. He insisted I phone him the minute I had any more information, even if it was the middle of the night, and I promised I would. After hanging up with Jeff, I paced the living room floor and waited for Anthony to come over and stand vigil with me till Jenny came home. When he arrived, he sat beside me on the couch. We exchanged our usual tortured psychoanalytical self-revelations, but tonight I had no stomach for it. I snapped at him, berated myself, apologized, and started to cry. Then I told Anthony I wanted to be alone.

"Are you sure?" he said. "I don't think I should leave you like this."

I nodded. I needed all my attention available to weave a psychic shield around my child, and Anthony was a distraction.

He kissed the top of my head and left.

For a while I sat on the couch in the dark and strained for the sound of tires on the gravel, signaling Jenny's return. I finally had to conclude that she wasn't coming home and that tomorrow could be a very long day. I would need all my strength to manage whatever came next. My body felt like Velcro as I ripped it from the couch. I dragged myself upstairs and climbed into bed with my clothes on, just in case I would need to get up in a hurry. I tried to stay awake and vigilant, but at last I succumbed to exhaustion and fell asleep.

●

Suddenly, I came fully awake in the dark, floating on a tide of wellbeing. It was as if I had stepped into a warm, well-lit cabin after being lost in a snowstorm in a dark forest. Like a deep drink of water after hiking up a ridge in the high desert, or finding out the tumor is benign and not malignant. Every fiber of my being relaxed and sighed with ease.

I heard a voice inside me say very calmly, "If Jenny dies tonight, it will be alright."

Permeated with that strange peace, I fell back to sleep and rested through the night.

By the next day, all equanimity had vanished, and it would be months before I remembered it even happened.

•

As soon as dawn began to lighten the horizon, I got up and called my mom. She tried to sound perky when she answered, but I could tell I had woken her.

"Mom . . . Jenny . . ." I could not utter another word. I was sobbing.

My mother had been tracking Jenny's unraveling since our return from Hawaii four days earlier. She had been propping me up with hopeful predictions about Jenny's return to her senses and reassurances that, while admittedly dramatic, Jenny's behavior fell into the spectrum of normal adolescent extremes.

Mom waited quietly for me to get a hold of myself, but I could feel the thrum of her anxiety across the phone line. "It's okay," she murmured. "Tell me what's going on."

I swallowed hard. "Jenny took off in my car last night. I don't know where she went. I don't know where she is. Mom, I'm so scared!"

"You went through this alone all night? Oh, my poor Mirabai! Why didn't you call me?"

"I didn't want to bother you. I thought she'd come back."

"I'll be right there."

Mom lived a half an hour away, but it felt like a decade before she pulled up to the house. Rightly suspecting that I would not eat of my own accord, she had brought me a breakfast burrito, which sat on the counter for the rest of the morning like an accusation. Food was for people who did not lose track of their children.

Mom sprang into action. She called Daniela and Amy, who cancelled all plans for the day and raced from their respective houses to see what they could do to help. Sean came over with his wife Tania, who often stayed with me when Sean went away on weekend Zen retreats, and they too dropped everything to sit with us while we tried to figure out how to find Jenny and get her back. We called the school to let them know that Jenny was missing, and they suspended classes for the day and organized search parties, spreading out across the county in a collective effort to locate my wayward girl. Every muscle in my body was coiled for action, but my team convinced me to stay home and wait in case Jenny came back.

Mom and Amy cleaned Jenny's messy room while I fought with the state police over the telephone. Local law enforcement had not done a thing to help. Nor were they willing to even begin until twenty-four hours had passed, at which time I was required to file an official missing person's report. Meanwhile, they had no record of Anthony's visit the night before, nor my follow-up call around midnight, nor my subsequent call early that morning, during which they had finally asked to stop calling.

"It's not our place to mediate family disputes, Ma'am," I was now being told.

"But it wasn't a dispute. My daughter is mentally ill. She is a danger to herself."

"It says here that she attacked you."

"No! Well, sort of. That was only part of what happened. She's having a psychotic break."

"There's nothing we can do about that, Ma'am."

"Hey, wait a minute, I thought you said you had no record of our report last night."

"It says here that you had a fight with your daughter and she fled in your blue Ford Escort."

"It wasn't a fight! And it was a purple Ford Explorer. Shit! You guys need to get your facts straight. Can't you send out an APB or something?"

"Please don't swear at me, Ma'am. You can file a report this evening. As I said."

"Right. Well."

The dispatcher hung up.

I clenched the phone, clenched my teeth, and roared into the empty air.

Tires on the gravel. I leapt from my chair. But it wasn't Jenny. It was the UPS truck, rumbling to a stop in front of the house. The horn honked, and Mom went outside to retrieve the delivery. It was a small box from my publisher. I set it unopened on the kitchen table. Mom picked it up.

"May I?"

I shrugged. "Go ahead."

A month earlier, before we went to Hawaii, the publisher had overnighted a glossy photocopy of the book cover. I wasn't home when the Fed-Ex package arrived. Jenny had opened it on her own and carefully resealed the envelope. Then, with the skill of a CIA operative, she spread Wite-Out over the return address and wrote in the name and address of Victoria's Secret, where I had been known to purchase the occasional item of lingerie. Only in addition to using the penmanship of a would-be physician, Jenny had spelled it "Victory's Secret." I pretended to be surprised and duly impressed by the ruse when she handed me the envelope after dinner that night.

Now my mother was opening the latest delivery from my publisher. Inside was an advance copy of my new translation of Dark Night of the Soul. In this moment my life's work felt like a cruel joke.

"Congratulations, Mirabai," my mother said.

"Congratulations," said my older daughter and my sister and the friends who had come over to keep me company as we waited for news of Jenny.

I glanced at the cover, flipped it over and took a look at the back, riffled through a few pages and set it on the table. Then I turned around and went back to staring out the window.

Half an hour later, the police pulled into the driveway.

CHAPTER 19

Her Chariot

I watched my reaction unfold like a traditional movie scene in which a mother receives the news that her child has been killed in an accident. As I saw myself prostrate on the porch floor, I reminded myself of Catholic nuns in the movies who prostrate themselves before the altar and cry out to Jesus. I reminded myself of myself as a small child, throwing myself on the kitchen floor and howling because my mother would not let me eat plain butter; once I had started crying, I was committed, and it had seemed wrong to stop. I reminded myself of Jenny laying herself flat before Maharaj-ji's tucket in full danda pranam.

"No," I whispered. And then I was wailing. "No!"

Couldn't I come up with something more original? Something more dignified?

"Mom! I need my mother!" I screamed.

"I'm right here, my love. I'm holding you." And she was. But I could not feel her arms wrapped around my torso, her face pressed against my face as she sobbed with me, our tears and teeth colliding in the storm.

And then I sat up. I mopped my tears with angry hands and lumbered to my feet. "Let's go," I said.

"We will accompany you to the funeral home," Officer Mora said, and for the first time his partner looked into my eyes and made a stab at a compassionate smile.

Funeral home. That sounded like a house, where people lived. Not a holding facility for dead bodies.

"Thank you," I said, and then I reached across the chasm of my own pain for Officer Mora's hand. "This must be very difficult for you to do," I said. "Is it . . . your first time?" He did not let me touch him.

"Not at all," he said. "I do this often." He pronounced the silent "t" in often, which bothered me. "It's my job."

"I see." So much for noble gestures. "Let me get my purse." But my purse had been in the car with Jenny. I had no purse. I turned in a helpless circle.

That's when I noticed Sean and Tania standing in the doorway, their faces collapsed in various versions of shock and mercy. I stepped inside, and they took turns embracing me, crooning, their eyes wild with sorrow.

"I need to call Jeff before we go." I had promised. And I wanted to feel the warmth of his voice enfolding me. But when he answered the phone on the first ring, I was detached. "Jenny's dead," I said bluntly.

And it was my steely Vietnam vet boyfriend who broke down.

"Mirabai, no!"

"I have to go. Identify her body." Still I did not cry.

"Oh, my love." It was late afternoon in New Mexico and early morning in Hawaii. Jeff was about to begin his workday, installing locks in a resort on Kauai. He had just been unloading his tools when I called. "I'm on my way." He threw everything back in the case and called a cab to the airport. Mom grabbed her keys, and I followed her to her car. Amy, who had just gone home to take a shower, magically reappeared in the back seat. She reached up and squeezed my shoulder in silence, and she did not let go. We followed the police car through town to the Rivera Family Mortuaries. We drove slowly, and the world held its breath as we passed. No mother should ever have to do this, I thought, and desperately wished that no other mother ever would. I will take this one, I said to the universe. Just don't make anyone else have to do identify the body of her child.

●

The medical investigator met us at the door. I knew her. We lifted weights together at the gym. Tenderly, she held my gaze for a moment.

"You ready?" Tamara asked. I bit my lip and nodded. "Please come with me," she said. And I followed the kindly coroner into a room in which, upon a cold metal table at its center, the body of my little girl lay.

I stood away for a moment, gazing from a distance, and then, as if wading into a pool of piranhas, I made my way to her.

She lay on her side, her body curled gently in on itself, like someone trying to find the perfect position to take a nap. Her eyes were slightly open, her lips barely parted. Her expression was settled, serene. Apart from a pale bruise on her cheek, she looked entirely unhurt, as if she had swallowed hemlock and not swerved and overcompensated, smashed a guardrail, tumbled across the sky, and flown through the shattered windshield before slamming to the ground beneath a ponderosa pine in a puddle of full moonlight.

You've gone too far this time, Jen.

But this was not the place to reprimand her, to criticize Jenny for dying and get her to promise never to die again.

I leaned over her and awkwardly wrapped my arms around her shoulders and bent to nuzzle her neck. I could not find my way around the foreign landscape of my daughter's dead body. It felt like I was walking in on an ancient esoteric rite in the inner sanctum of a goddess temple, and so I withdrew from this one-sided embrace.

I stood up and opened the palms of my hands. "Fly with angels, my love." And I turned and walked away from the empty vessel that used to hold Jenny's life force.

Fucking angels. I did not want to give them my daughter. But it was evident that I had no choice. And something in me seemed to get that my highest task at this moment was to love her enough to release her into their waiting wings, where they would lift her and exalt her, and carry her away from me forever, and keep her safe.

●

"She heard the call and she went running," Jeff said when he returned from Hawaii and drove over to the funeral home to view her body. "And her chariot came back empty."

CHAPTER 20

Kaddish, etc.

Again they took her away. Now that I had found her, even if only her empty shell, I couldn't bear to let her out of my sight. But because Jenny died alone (they told me), she had to have an autopsy. State law (they told me). Later I found out that, as Jenny's mother, I had the right to decide whether or not a team of strangers could slice open the cavity of my daughter's body-temple and weigh, measure, and otherwise intrude upon her ruined organs. But I did not know this at the time, and I let them separate us. I comforted myself with the thought that Jenny, a budding scientist, would have been fascinated by notion of peeling away the outer covering to reveal the inner architecture of the human form.

News of Jenny's death swiftly permeated the fabric of the community and drenched it with the weight of collective mourning. The house began to fill with close friends and friendly acquaintances. Framed photos of Jenny I didn't even know existed appeared nestled between pots of soup and armfuls of flowers. As if engaged in a deadly game of chess, Mom assessed each new offering and placed it with care, as if by creating order amid the chaos of loss she might prevent my annihilation. But nothing could save me from that fire. It swept through the landscape of what had been my life and took everything to the ground.

I sat among the wreckage. I rent my garment. I fasted and groaned and stared into space. I let myself burn, melt, distort and dissolve. Why not? I had nothing more to lose.

Although every one of the religions and spiritual paths I once knew and loved now struck me as ludicrous, Judaism and Buddhism seemed to offer the most robust containers in which to hold this impossible thing. I re-read the Tibetan Book of the Dead and committed myself to accompanying Jenny's soul through the Bardos with forty-nine days of prayer. Just in case there was any such thing as a soul. And just in case there was a metaphysical topography that my daughter's soul was now navigating. On her own. Without me to guide and protect her.

My friend Annapurna, another of many Jews in our circle of monkey worshippers, had attended rabbinical school, so I asked her about mourning rituals from my ancestral tradition. She opened a sacred toolbox I had not known was there. We draped the mirrors with cloth so that I would not have to see the face of my anguish. I tore the collar of my favorite purple blouse and wore it to remind me of the built-in obsolescence of this material world. I slid from my position on the couch and onto the floor, because all the furniture of the life I knew had been removed, and there was nowhere to sit but in the emptiness.

And so, we sat shiva. Every day for seven days at sunset, visitors arrived in droves, and we chanted the Kaddish together. Then, leaving miso soup (which I could not swallow) or books on grief (which I did not even open), they went away.

At first I was perplexed and eventually relieved by the fact that the traditional Jewish mourner's prayer does not even mention death. Instead the Kaddish extolls the majesty of the Holy One and kindles awe in Its glorious unknowability. Annapurna made photocopies of the transliterated Aramaic, along with an inclusive English translation, and put out the call for anyone who wanted to join us in the ancient liturgy. Jews and Gentiles, pagans and atheists, sat on the floor with me, praising God in honor of my daughter. It made no sense, but we all came away feeling blessed.

Let the Great Name be blessed forever and ever.

Let the Name of the Source of Life be glorified, exalted, honored,

though the One is beyond all the praises, songs
and adorations we can utter.
And let us say, Amen.

●

Meanwhile, the moment our satsang heard that Jenny had died, they gathered at the Hanuman temple and commenced to sing the 108 Hanuman Chaleesas to help her on her spirit journey. Teams of devotees took turns chanting all afternoon and through the night. Mom drove me over to the ashram at dawn that first morning after Jenny's death. We entered the temple as the last few verses of the chaleesas were being sung and the singers were heading home to bed. Silent hugs, soft sobs, flowers pressed into my hands. I lay my head on Maharaj-ji's tucket, cursed him and forgave him, told him I thought he was a fraud and threw myself at his invisible feet, begging him to keep my baby safe. Then I went back home and stayed there.

Every once a while I tipped my head backwards against the couch and moaned. "Oh, Jenny, no." Or "I don't know how to do this." Which seemed to cause some of my companions to panic a little.

"You're not supposed to do anything, Mirabai," someone would inevitably explain to me.

They didn't get it. What I meant was that I didn't know how to live the next minute now that Jenny's minutes had come to a halt. I didn't know how I could possibly breathe my next involuntary breath when my daughter had abruptly ceased breathing. I didn't know if I could continue showing up since I had failed the primal mission: keeping my child alive.

●

Jeff flew all night from the Islands and met up with Roy at the Albuquerque airport, and they drove home together through the mountains to Taos. When they pulled in around six on the evening of the day after Jenny's body was found, they were confused by the cars that lined both sides of the driveway and spilled out to the edges of Maestas Road for nearly a block in each direction. It was the mourners—dozens of them—gathered for Kaddish.

Roy and Jeff had to pick their way through the throng of kneeling worshippers to reach me. My brother hugged me and then released me into my lover's arms, where I finally wept.

May the Source of Life
Who causes peace to reign in the high heavens
Let peace descend upon us,
And on all beings.
And let us say, Amen.

It wasn't enough to pray and wail and receive condolences. There were arrangements to be made.

While the office of the medical investigator (OMI) was investigating the cause of my daughter's death down in Albuquerque, and Jeff and Roy were flying over the Mohave, and friends were bustling about the house, arranging flowers and rearranging the contents of the refrigerator, Mom, Amy, Daniela, and I had been meeting with Tim, the director of Rivera's funeral home.

"This is fucked up," I declared to Tim. "Making decisions like this. I'm sorry, but this fucking sucks."

He did not flinch. "I know," he agreed. "It sucks."

A circle of seven women met the OMI van when it pulled in from Albuquerque the next day, bearing the body of my little girl. They wheeled her into a little room on the side of the mortuary and closed the door. And there they prepared her body for its final homecoming.

I will never know exactly what unfolded beneath their brave and generous hands. How they rubbed lavender oil into her cold skin and sprinkled her with rosewater. How they combed her brown and purple curls with their fingertips and pressed shut her eyelids and her lips. How they navigated the rough-stitched incision that ran from her clavicle to her pelvis, lifting her new woman hips and adjusting her shoulders as they washed and anointed her. How they sang to her in harmony, in unison, and alone. Hebrew prayers, Arabic. Hindu chants and Buddhist sutras. How they read the psalms and the poems of Emily Dickenson and Shakespearean soliloquies.

Women whose daughters had played with my daughters. Women I did not know well, but who knew well how to prepare a body in the tradition of my ancestors. Women I had been writing with in an intimate group for almost a decade. Who, every week, gathered at one or another of our homes to take turns as our guide for that day: read a poem; pull a line; go. Writing through the surface of our minds to that deeper, quieter, truer place. Never commenting, critiquing, analyzing. Simply thanking each writer after she read her piece aloud, sometimes through tears, and moving on to the next. Just as Natalie Goldberg, our group's founder, had taught us. Never had I felt so deeply supported than I had in my silent writer's group. Now these companions were showing up to accomplish the impossible task of preparing my daughter's dead body.

I needed to bring her home. Anthony stayed up all night carving an open casket of Spanish cedar. Jack borrowed a low carved table from an antique dealer and set it up in our living room as a pedestal. I did not want her body to be transported to our home in a hearse, so Johnno offered the use of his covered pickup, which he and Roy hosed out and then lined with flowers. Other friends gathered armfuls of juniper boughs and bundles of sage to surround her.

When preparations were complete, I climbed into the back of the truck and rode home with her. I rested my hand on her waxen forehead, and I sang the little song I had made up and sang a thousand nights to help her fall asleep when she was small, a Spanish nursery rhyme I had put to music:

Duérmete, my niña.

Duérmete, mi sol.

Duérmete, pedazo de mi corazón.

Sleep, my child.

Sleep, my sunshine.

Sleep, you piece of my heart.

"It looks like a cradle," someone said, when we had lifted Jenny's casket from the pickup, carried it inside, and laid it on the bier.

And it did.

Jenny Bird handed me a basket of flowers and evergreen branches. "Why don't you arrange them around her?"

Decorate my daughter? Suddenly this seemed as daunting as identifying her body. I had the urge to run away. Please, someone else, do this beautiful thing. I will watch. I will be grateful. I cannot lift my arm. Let me rest. Make it stop.

I reached into the basket. I spread a blanket of pine boughs and carnations around the base of the cradle. I tucked a bouquet of apricot rose buds into the folds of Jenny's blue dolphin shroud. I circled her head with baby's breath and placed marigolds at her feet and hands. When I had used up one armload, another was handed to me, until I had woven a tapestry of color and texture, light and fragrance, around Jenny's body as she lay in state in front of the west-facing window of the home where we had lived together.

And while I worked, Jenny Bird sang the song Jenny Starr had loved to hear her sing: "Ave Maria." She sang like an angel, calling on the angels to gather, to be with us, to spread over us a mantel of goodness and lull this child to sleep, to rest, to rest in peace. Hail Mary, full of grace. Calling on the Blessed Mother to be with us in our hour of need, to stay with us forever, because we would never again not need her grace.

My friend Father Bill—who was later to become one of the closest soul companions I have ever had—came to anoint Jenny's body, and he wove teachings from Tibet with the sacrament of Rome. "Go toward the light," he prayed. "Do not be afraid. Merge into the light."

My sister's young sons did not leave their cousin's side. Nick stood over the casket and stared at her, as if watching for signs that she might still be breathing, and, concluding that she would never breathe again, he sobbed. Ian climbed into my lap as I sat on the floor. "I just thought you might need to hold a child right now," he said and leaned back against me so that I had no choice but to wrap my arms around him and rock.

•

The phone rang, and I saw "Richard Alpert" flash across the caller ID. I picked it up.

"Mirabai, it's Ram Dass."

I did not burst into tears. I was as still as snow. "Thank you for calling."

"John told me what happened." His voice was bumpy from his stroke a few years earlier. I softened into the quiet between the words. "About how she . . . the Mother . . . the grace."

"Yes, it started during Durga Puja. She was acting like a goddess. People were touching her feet."

"Yes."

"I didn't like that."

"No."

"She was not the Divine Mother, Ram Dass. She was my little girl. She was going crazy."

"Both," he said.

"Yes. But still."

"I know." Ram Dass told me a story about a time in the early seventies when he was giving a talk at Saint John of the Divine Church in New York City, and hundreds of people had come to listen, and they were all meditating and chanting, and Ram Dass's father stood in the back with his stepmother. At one point the Jewish business tycoon turned to his wife and said, "I feel like the goddamned Virgin Mary."

Ram Dass and I both laughed, and the irreverence felt good. And then he said, "Mirabai, the energy that came pouring through Jenny was too much for her body to contain, and she shattered."

That's exactly how it had felt to me.

"Look. Jenny was the same age when she died as you were when you started your spiritual path," Ram Dass said.

He had been there. He remembered.

"And now you will take up the dharma for both of you."

I thanked him, and we sat in silence for a moment across the miles. "I want to know if she's all right," I said.

"She's under Baba's blanket, and all is well," Ram Dass said. "And you are a mother who has lost a child, and that will never be all right."

Jenny's friends brought special objects to be burned with her. Poems they had written and watercolors they had painted, Calvin and Hobbes cartoons, the roach of a joint, a tiny carving of Kuan Yin. When they had finished making their offerings, they drifted into her room and closed the door. I could hear them in there, playing Jenny's favorite music on her stereo, going through her clothes and her bumper stickers and her prayer beads.

"Take what you want," I blurted, and so they did, and then it was gone, and then I wanted it back, but it was too late.

Finally, Kali appeared, guarded by her mother. She stood at the foot of Jenny's casket for a long time, her expression veiled. But when Kali's father saw her beholding her dead soul sister for the first time, a tortured sob erupted from the ground of his being. He stood behind me, his arms wrapped around my chest, and buried his face in my hair. Everyone paused and held what was left of our family in sacred silence. There was nothing to be said.

"These people are energy vampires," Kali's mother blurted out. "They're just getting off on the drama." And she whisked her daughter away.

But I did not question their motives. Each body that walked through that door belonged to a hand that kept me from drowning. And they continued to gather through the evening. We pushed the living room furniture back against the walls, and my mom had a room-sized Zapotec rug brought over from her gallery so we could sit at Jenny's feet all night long. I wanted to send her on her way to the next world on the wings of song. We prayed and chanted from sunset to sunrise, in Sanskrit and Tibetan, Hebrew and Arabic and Latin, Lakota and Tiwa and English and Greek. We sat apart, and we wept in each other's arms. Candles, incense, flowers, pots of tea and boxes of dark chocolate, a bottle of mescal and bowls of guacamole and chips. We passed around the photo album Amy and Daniela had spent all day creating, and we marveled at the incredibly alive pictures of Jenny through every year of her incandescent little incarnation.

•

By the time the edges of the landscape began to take shape in the early morning light, the last of the mourners who had kept vigil with us all through the night drifted back home, and for a few minutes Jeff and I were alone with Jenny. We took our seats beside her body and sat together in silence. Soon, my mom drove up with Amy and Roy, followed by Daniela. We all sat around her for a little longer, sipping our coffee and prolonging the illusion that she was still with us. Then, with the help of a few strong friends who materialized to help us carry her casket back outside, we loaded her back into the truck to be transported to the crematorium in Española.

In a guttural voice that rose from the chasm of my loins and did not seem to belong to me, I led the funeral procession through the garden, chanting the Buddhist sutra I had learned when I was Jenny's age:

Gate gate paragate parasamgate
Bodhi Swaha!

•

Gone. Gone beyond. Gone beyond the beyond.
All hail to the one who goes!

Practicing letting go. Practicing bowing at the feet of the mystery. Practicing saying yes when every cell in my body was screaming NO.

We loaded Jenny's body into the truck and once again I climbed in and settled beside her. We drove south, dipping down into the Rio Grande Gorge, and winding our way along the river canyon. Jeff sang through the forty-five miles to the crematorium: Sri Ram Jai Ram Jai Jai Ram.

When we arrived, we informed the staff that we would like to accompany Jenny's body to point where it was delivered into the furnace. They countered by informing us that this was not usually done, and furthermore they had another cremation scheduled in an hour, so there was no time to linger. We agreed, and we followed a thin man with a straw hat that darkened a face like the desert.

"Vengan conmigo."

He led us into a cavernous chamber, where he opened a vault in the wall and slid out a concrete slab. This, apparently, was where we were meant to deposit the sacred flesh of my child. The cremation technician helped us to lift the casket onto the sliding base.

"No cabe," he said, shaking his head apologetically. "Es muy grande." He patted the carved end of Jenny's cedar cradle by way of explanation. Then he disappeared for a moment and returned with a bow saw.

"Se puede?" he asked me, and I nodded.

He began to saw off the beautiful arc of Jenny's beautiful casket, and I began to laugh. The thin man checked to see if I was becoming hysterical, then glanced at my loved ones, who had begun to laugh too. He shrugged and proceeded to saw. And while he worked, we rubbed each other's backs and wiped our eyes and collected ourselves.

When he was finished, she fit perfectly.

I took one last look at my child and said, in Spanish, "She looks like the Virgin of Guadalupe, doesn't she? Draped in blue, surrounded with red roses."

The cremator nodded, touched his hand to his heart, and began to push her into the empty chamber.

"Espere," I said, and he paused. I took the mala from around my neck, the string of 108 prayer beads Ram Dass had given me when I was Jenny's age, a thread of Maharaj-ji's blanket tucked inside the amber guru-bead, and I placed it around my daughter's shrouded head.

"Okay," I said.

"Wait!" Now it was Roy's turn to halt the process. "Can my sister press the button?" The longsuffering attendant stared at Roy, either not comprehending the question or else utterly perplexed by it. Roy took my hand. "Do you want to, Mirabai? Do you want to . . . start the fire?"

I had identified my daughter's body at the morgue. I had decorated it with blossoms and greens. I had lain all night beside her. I could do this too. Suddenly I knew that I needed to do this too. Silently, I blessed my brother for suggesting this outrageous and courageous thing, and I stepped up.

Together, as a family, we leaned in and pushed Jenny's body along the rollers and into the furnace. The thin man closed the door, and I peered through the smudged window.

After looking one by one at the people who loved me most, I turned and pressed the button that ignited the flames, which exploded in an audible rush and turned my daughter's body into fire, and then to dust.

CHAPTER 21

Scattering

They surrounded me like a peasant militia trying to defend a village from an imperialist army. But no matter how valiantly my loved ones fought to protect me against the violence of my loss, they could not shield me from the inevitable. What I needed, in fact, was a moment alone so that I could begin to take in and integrate with what had happened.

A few days after Jenny's death, I convinced everyone that I would be fine on my own for a little while, and I finally had an hour to myself. I lay down on the floor and took up the work of grieving. I watched as a wall of pain rose above me, and I understood that I was powerless to get out of its path. So I surrendered and allowed it to wash over me like a tidal wave. I was willing to be obliterated. I had nothing to lose.

Even as I rocked on my knees, howling, I detected soft breathing behind the roaring. I leaned in, listened. It was the murmuring of ten million mothers, backward and forward in time and right now, who had also lost children. They were lifting me, holding me. They had woven a net of their broken hearts, and they were keeping me safe there. I realized that one day I would take my rightful place as a link in this web, and I would hold my sister-mothers when their children died. For now my only task was to grieve and be cradled in their love.

•

Jenny's ashes came back to me in a box of handmade paper, dyed blue-green, studded with flower seeds. An eco-friendly urn! Designed to be buried, where it would melt back into the earth and give rise to new life. Whatever. I wasn't letting that container out of my sight. I didn't want anyone else to touch it, either, except family members and maybe a close friend if I was in the mood. Jenny's remains were all that remained. That and her toothbrush, which sat in its ceramic cup in the downstairs bathroom like the white flag of surrender.

My pain was my connection to my child, and no one was going to get away with spouting platitudes in my presence: "Time heals all wounds." Or, "Now she is an angel." Or, "She is no longer suffering." And this one: "You must get on with your life." If soothing the fire of grief meant I would no longer be able to feel my baby girl, then let me burn. Plus, I wasn't interested in parenting an angel. Also, Jenny had not been suffering; she was having a human experience. And what was this life I was supposed to be getting on with? I had died with my daughter. My old life was over, and I had no interest in cultivating a new one.

Nothing pleased me; no one could say the right thing. I tried to be polite. I could feel the awkwardness of acquaintances as they tried to express their condolences, and I did my best to rescue them, thanking them for their sympathy. But my tolerance for anything less than searing authenticity was about zero. On the other hand, when people didn't say anything at all, I was outraged. There were old friends and colleagues who never sent a note or picked up the phone, and I couldn't believe it. Cowards, I concluded. They did not have the guts to step into the shattered landscape of a mother's heart.

And then there were all the other moments—moments when my judgments and cravings fell away—and I simply sat with my loss and allowed myself to become acquainted with my desolation. "It's just unbearable anguish" became my mantra, which I uttered silently and with an ironic smile whenever the pain came at me like a freight train. Then I lay down in its tracks and investigated what it felt like to be run over.

As I learned to abide in the wreckage, a realization began to grow in me: You are shattered, yes, said my inner voice. Do not be in a rush to put the pieces back together. Go ahead and be nobody for as long as you can.

And so I did.

•

The day of the memorial service was uncommonly balmy. Early November in the Sangre de Cristo Mountains is supposed to be cold and gray. It should have been snowing by now, but the sky was so blue it was almost violet, and flocks of birds shot across the sky and landed among the dried gardens of the Hanuman temple, where the service was to take place. I wore Jenny's blue velvet dress, which was two sizes too big for me. How had my gangly little girl blossomed into a voluptuous young woman? A young woman now made of ash in a box on an altar in this strange sunshine.

In honor of Jenny's love of the color blue, almost everyone turned up in various shades of blue clothing. Natalie, who had never had a pedicure in her life, accompanied me to the nail salon the day before, and we both emerged with blue toes. Ashram cooks sprinkled blue food coloring into the rice, the cake, the chai. Blue balloons were tied to every tree, and the tables outside were draped in blue silk.

Vishu sang chaleesas, and Nancy played her Native flute. Elaine was the emcee, and Amy was the first the speak, sharing recollections of her niece as the imp she could be, confessing to serving Jenny bowls of Lucky Charms cereal whenever she slept over, since Auntie Amy knew she would never get such forbidden fruits at my house. I miraculously made it through reading the eulogy I had miraculously managed to compose the day before.

"And now," Elaine said, "if there is anyone who feels moved to share a prayer or memories of Jenny, we invite you to come up."

That's when I discovered that an open mic situation at a funeral is not a great idea--unless you are willing to sit for a very long time. Adult after adult came forward and told long stories about my child's childhood and sang every verse of "Amazing Grace." I looked around for Kali and Jessie, but not one of Jenny's closest friends was sitting with us. None of them stepped up to the mic and spoke about the impact this person had on their life, or revealed how her death had ruptured the most tender membrane of their heart, or allowed us to bear witness to their wondering how the hell they were supposed to finish growing up without her. Instead, the teenagers milled around the ashram grounds like phantoms, casting sideways glances toward the ceremony—almost accusatory, as if we were doing it all wrong—and refused to participate.

The late autumn sun seared my face as I took in the testimonies of the people Jenny touched. Teachers from preschool through high school spoke about whichever unique developmental phase unfolded under their watch. Satsang members confessed that, although they were certain she was with Maharaj-ji now, they would prefer to have her with us. Then someone recited a Rumi poem. And then someone else offered cornmeal and tobacco to the seven directions. Others tried to speak, but could only weep and sat back down. This tragedy had shredded the fabric of our community, and everything spilled from the open seams.

Finally, we sang a Hanuman Chaleesa, did aarti, offering the light to the photographs of Jenny and Maharaj-ji that flanked her ashes, and it was over. Then came the long line of well-wishers. I sat in my little folding chair and received each one—the hugs, the clasped hand, the offers of massage and tapping therapy and retreats on remote islands in the South Pacific. There were old friends I hardly recognized through the smoke from my grief fire. I smiled and thanked them and hoped no one would feel dissed by my daze.

●

The day after the memorial service—eleven days after Jenny was found dead by a road crew at the bottom of an embankment off Highway 518—Jeff and I flew to Hawaii. The hotel in Kauai where Jeff had been working when Jenny died had saved his job for him to finish up once he had attended to his family crisis. And there were three more installations waiting behind that one. As a sympathy offering, his company paid for me to accompany him back to Hawaii. It made sense for me to go. I couldn't pay homage to the sacred mystery unfolding amid the familiar furniture of my forever-transfigured old life.

I carried some of Jenny's ashes in a zip lock bag inside a Guatemalan purse, which I wore around my neck. When the guard at the Albuquerque airport tried to take it from me in the security line, my voice instantly escalated in pitch and caliber. "This is what's left of my daughter," I declared. "She's staying with me."

He did not relent.

I had anticipated this possibility, and I was prepared. "I have her death certificate right here." I reached into the woven bag and pulled out the document.

The guard ignored me and signaled for reinforcements, who unceremoniously lifted the purse from my body and placed it on the conveyer belt. I burst into tears, rushed through the screening, and grabbed my bag of ashes before it had the chance to be touched by another officious person who did not give a shit about me or Jenny or the sacred bits of ash and bone that were all that remained of the most alive person I had ever known.

●

Unlike during my first trip to Hawaii a little more than two weeks earlier, this time the beauty of the islands was like a brittle film over my eyes. It kept dissolving beneath my gaze. I would stare at the contours of the surf, and I could not focus. We would hike up into the volcanic mountains, and even as I sat amid a hedge of pink and yellow wildflowers and looked down on miles of verdant hills unrolling to the coast, I could not see what I was seeing. This is beautiful, I would inform myself. But beautiful was just a word.

We drove for hours up a winding dirt road to a remote Shiva temple, where we asked the pujari there to make an offering for our dead daughter. And then we returned to the hotel and got to work. I strapped on my lock-installer's-assistant tool belt, stuck my cordless drill in the loop, arranged the bits in the drill-bit pockets, and did my job, stripping lock after lock down the long corridor of a tropical resort. At first I tried to offer a prayer for Jenny's journey with each fresh door. But then I surrendered to the numbing monotony of the job and gave thanks for the sanctuary it offered.

At the end of the day, my feet were so tired I could hardly walk, my forearm vibrated from pressing against all those door jambs with my heavy drill, and I was hungry for the first time since Jenny died. For food. For mai-tais. For sex. And for a perilous adventure.

•

We took a week off to visit Ben and Martha, Jeff's brother and sister-in-law, who were caretakers for a small timeshare complex on the beach in Maui. They invited us to stay in one of the second-story units that overlooked the fountain and gardens Ben had crafted and cultivated during his decade as the groundskeeper. Martha filled our apartment with baskets of pineapple and mango, roasted macadamia nuts and sprays of plumeria blossoms. Ben offered to take us to a secret spot along the road to Hanna, where we could leap into a series of volcanic pools that spilled from one to the other down a succession of thirty and forty-foot bluffs.

I did not give it a second thought. I would be leaping.

This was unlike me, but I was no longer the person who trembled at heights and panicked in deep water. And besides, the last shred of self-preservation had been torn from me when Jenny died. Daniela was a mother herself and no longer needed me. I had no need to keep myself safe. The worst that would happen is that I would split my head open on the rocks as I plummeted downward. Oh well.

We stood on the first ledge, and I stared down into the black pool far below. "How do we get back up?" I casually inquired.

"There's a trail at the bottom," Ben said. "But once you jump into the first pool, you're committed. The only way out is to swim across and jump off the next one until you reach the last one. I'll meet you guys at the end."

I gazed out across the acres of rainforest, gauging how far I would have to swim until my feet found solid purchase on the other shore of the first pool. Far.

"You don't have to do this," Ben said.

"She can do it," said his brother. "Right, Mirabai?"

I jumped.

Without any special prayers or preparations, I bent my knees and propelled myself as far away from the edge of the cliff as I could. I flew through the air, the cliff sides streaming past my shoulders, and I bellowed.

"This is for you, Jen!"

I hit the water, shot deep below the surface, and then swam upward. Just as I broke through, Jeff dove in beside me, and there we were in the belly of the jungle, held in her womb, sputtering and laughing. The dark canyon walls surged around us, passionflower vines spilling down their long face. I swam to the other side and jumped again. And again. Four times.

Jenny would have been proud of me. Jenny would have been amazed.

•

Between electronic lock installations on Maui and Kauai, we offered Jenny's ashes in the temple of nature. At La Perouse we navigated a field of sharp volcanic rock, and I tossed the first handful of my cremated child into the surf and waited. This was a dolphin habitat, and Jenny loved dolphins. I was certain they would come to greet us and carry my little girl out to the sea.

Nothing.

Feeling personally abandoned by the porpoise community, I walked slowly behind Jeff as we headed back to the car.

"Mirabai, look!" Jeff turned and pointed to the shore break. There they were—a pod of dolphins—leaping and arcing through the waves.

"Thanks, guys," I whispered.

At the end of the long dock in Hanalei Bay, Jeff knelt, stretching out his arms to toss Jenny's cremains into the ocean, when suddenly a wave rose and crashed against the pilings and washed the ashes out of his hands. It was as if the Pacific had said, "I'll take that, thank you." He laughed and let go.

Sometimes while Jeff was working, I would wander away from the job site and down to the beach. I sat and stared at the horizon, or curled up in fetal position and nestled into the sand. Sometimes I dozed off. I was amazed by how much energy it took to grieve. I was exhausted all the time, as if I were bleeding internally and growing anemic, but there were no outward signs to justify my complete lack of energy.

On one such afternoon, as I lay in the warm sand and started to let myself slip into the comfort of oblivion, I suddenly had a thought that caused me to bolt upright: this was the longest Jenny and I had ever been apart. My heart welled with unspent parenting, like a nursing mother whose overfull breasts ache when she is separated from her baby. It felt like one of those dreams where you accidentally leave your kid at the gas station and don't realize until the next day, and then when you go back to look for her, she is gone.

This was followed by another excruciating epiphany: when I get home to Taos, I will be the mother of the dead girl.

A cascade of panicky notions unfurled from that one: Wherever I go, people will look at me sorrowfully, strain to say the right thing, or avoid me at the post office as if they might catch the dead-child disease if they met my eyes. They will wonder if Jenny and I had fought before her accident. If it was my fault. They will speculate that she was drinking, using drugs, out of control. They will feel sorry for me. I will hate that most of all: the overly sweetened tincture of their pity.

I couldn't face my community. I didn't want to go home. What kind of home did I have to go to? I had been in the middle of being Jenny's mother, and suddenly I was finished. How could I go grocery shopping when Jenny's special items—Thai noodles, turkey jerky, Nutella—were not on the list?

I realized that I had been completely codependent in my relationship with Jenny. That I needed her like a plant needs oxygen for photosynthesis. That although a parent is supposed to be the source of support for the child, Jenny had, in fact, been the ground upon which

I had built my life. With her death, the foundation was shattered. I had nothing to stand on. My existence was in free fall. Jenny had been my safety net; now all safety was gone.

This realization staggered me. I took it in. I sat there on the beach, and I took that knowledge all the way in.

•

When we returned to Taos, I hid in my house. I had an excuse. I was observing a year of ritual mourning in the Jewish tradition, which specifies that the people closest to the deceased refrain from engaging in anything that is not absolutely necessary for twelve months following the death of their loved one. This meant leaving the house only to go to work and preferably getting others to handle your basic errands. It meant not socializing—no parties or dinners out, no weddings or birthday celebrations. This gives the bereaved an opportunity to be fully present with what happened and to honor their beloved dead with undivided attention.

Friends took over my classes at the university to finish the semester, and my work as a translator did not require that I travel any further than from my bed to my desk. Although I was committed to showing up for the process of grief, there were times when I needed a break, an escape.

One night, when I was feeling stir-crazy, Jeff said, "Let's go to a movie."

"I don't want to see anybody," I said. "I don't want to be seen."

"Wear dark glasses."

"Ha ha." But a movie was exactly what I wanted. I could slide down low in my seat and melt into those giant faces, those bright landscapes, those fictitious people's pain. "Okay. Let's go."

I don't recall what the movie was—some kind of Indie film, with a dark adolescent having an existential crisis. I didn't care. I just wanted to forget for a moment. It was working, until the scene in which the protagonist had a vision of his grandfather appearing at the foot of his bed in the middle of the night and telling him he loved him. In the morning, the movie boy found out that his grandpa had died in the night. He had come to his grandson to bid him farewell!

As we drove home, I started to rant.

"I hate that shit," I yelled. "Dead people coming to tell their loved ones goodbye." I tried to snort with contempt, but instead I burst into tears. "Why didn't Jenny come to me?" I sobbed. "Why do the spirits of dead people come to everyone else? What's wrong with me?" I was pounding the door with the side of my fist. Jeff drove in broken-hearted consternation.

As we unlocked the house, walked inside, and turned on the lights, I suddenly remembered the night that Jenny died—only I hadn't known that yet—when I had fallen asleep waiting for her and then was suddenly awakened by that wave of peace.

That was her goodbye! Enfolding me in the wings of a deeper peace than I had ever known. No concepts, no images—simply a profound silence, an unshakable stillness, complete equanimity.

In that moment, standing in our quiet kitchen, my fury drained, and I felt fully blessed. I closed my eyes and reached out to my invisible daughter. "Thanks, Jen," I whispered.

"Oh, Mom," I felt her reply.

CHAPTER 22

Yahrtzeit

On the day of the unveiling it was snowing. Heavy, wet flakes had been falling on and off for days, melting the minute they landed, turning the high desert into a bayou. We pushed Jenny's headstone in a wheelbarrow from the parking lot to the Lama burial gardens, where Jeff had excavated a small hole to bury the box that contained the remaining half of Jenny's ashes.

The other half had been scattered all over the earth—in places Jenny had always wanted to visit. Ram Rani had taken the first packet to India where, with the blessing of Siddhi Ma and the ritual support of a team of Brahmin priests, they released them into the little river that borders Maharaj-ji's ashram in the foothills of the Himalayas. Daniela and her children had climbed with me to the top of the John Dunn Bridge overlooking the spot where Jenny first began to slip away from this world, and we each took turns dropping a handful of Jenny dust into the swirling confluence. Fernando had rented a boat in Puerto Morelos so we could toss Jenny's remains into the Caribbean along with armfuls of hibiscus blossoms. My mom, Ramón, and Mom's new partner, John, accompanied us to a quiet cove on Laguna Bacalar, where Mallina and Atzin conducted a Mesoamerican ceremony, burning copal in an earthenware bowl, and, punctuated with blasts of a conch shell, calling upon the spirits of the ancestors to receive our precious child. Jeff and Kali planted an aspen tree outside the window of Kali's old room and sprinkled a handful of ashes into the soil as they spaded and patted the earth around it. Lama was to be the final sacred space.

I had chosen a spot beneath a half-burnt ponderosa pine at the far northwestern edge of the Lama property. I wanted a remote place where I could escape and grieve and remember my daughter in solitude over the remaining years of my life. But on this late October afternoon, high in the mountains, surrounded by a band of loyal friends and relatives, I realized how impractical this spot was. If it weren't for Jeff, I might never have even found it again. Plus, it was starting to snow, which transfigured any familiar landmarks.

Our little group trudged faithfully alongside me as we bushwhacked through the scrub oak. Some carried musical instruments—drums and bells and a tanpura—and others brought stones and shells to encircle the new grave. Almost none of Jenny's friends were there; no girls— just a couple of boys I hardly knew, plus Jenny's friend Sam, who played the piano like a reincarnation of Mozart crossed with Keith Jarret. Everyone else was connected to me personally or to us as a family. Once again I was struck by how all the kids who had grown up around my kitchen table had seemingly evaporated in the firestorm of Jenny's death.

We gathered at the gravesite and stood in spontaneous silence for a few minutes. My sister placed the handmade paper urn in my hands, and I lowered it into the opening. Then, while chanting Hebrew prayers and drumming for Mother Earth, we all took turns throwing handfuls of soil on top. When the tomb was filled, Jeff lifted the head-stone and wedged it into the earth. It had been exactly one year since Jenny lost her mind and raced over the mountain to her death. Now, amid diagonal snowfall shot with sunlight, our improvised Yahrtzeit was complete.

I bowed at the foot of the grave and inhaled. Then I sat on my knees, and I tried to sing my daughter her final lullaby, the song my own mother had sung to us throughout our childhood. "I gave my love a cherry without a stone . . . ." But I began to quaver on the second verse: "How can there be a story that has no end?" And by the time I got to the last verse, I could not finish: "A baby when she's sleeping, there's no cryin'."

A strong wind gusted as we packed up our tools and instruments.

Jeff patted a few loose clods around our daughter's gravestone. Then he held my gloved hand in his gloved hand, and we headed down to Lama central to warm up with the bowls of soup and loaves of fresh bread the community had prepared for us.

•

Our decision to get married had been an effort to give me something wonderful so that I could survive the first anniversary. Jeff thinks it was his idea. I know it was mine. One day I was talking with my therapist, who was trying to help me to navigate the wilderness into which Jenny's death had plunged me.

"What do you really want?" he asked. "Besides getting your daughter back."

"To get married," I whispered, my head bowed. I might as well have confessed a desire to conquer Mexico for the shame I felt in admitting this.

"What's wrong with that?" Dr. Sargent asked.

"Jeff feels like we're already married, and he doesn't need the approval of the government."

"How do you feel?"

"Like I'm drowning in fire and being married to Jeff would be a cool island where I could find refuge."

"Then go home and tell him."

That evening, when Jeff returned from a job out of town, I was making dinner.

"Hi, Honey. I'd like to get married in the fall," I blurted out, before he had even had a chance to wash his hands and get down the salad bowl from the high cupboard.

"OK," Jeff said and promptly dropped to his knees at my feet. He removed the avocado and the knife from my hand and set them on the cutting board beside me. Then he wrapped his arms around my waist and looked up into my eyes. "Mirabai, will you marry me?"

Just like that. We were engaged. I was still bobbing on waves of flame, but in the distance a boat was sailing toward me, and the captain was calling my name.

●

At the same time that we were planning our wedding, we were picking out our child's gravestone. I searched the classified section of the newspaper and found someone advertising hand-carved memorial markers. Mr. Martinez agreed to drop by my house the following afternoon with his portfolio.

"I'm sorry for your loss," he said, as we shook hands. "Me and my wife lost our baby back in sixty-nine. That's how I got into this line of work."

"I'm sorry for your loss, too," I said.

"That's okay. It was a long time ago."

I tried to visualize myself at eighty, Jenny's death four decades behind me, a tender ember of melancholy, rather than a raging bonfire of anguish. I couldn't do it.

We looked through photographs of ornate stone memorials, bordered by carved angels and crosses and curlicues. I hated them all. They had nothing to do with my quirky, iconoclastic girl.

"Can't I do something simple?" I asked. "Something more . . . contemporary?"

"Sure enough!" Mr. Martinez showed me a list of fonts, inviting me to pick one and compose my own inscription. "You could say, 'In loving memory of our dearly departed Jennifer Nicole Starr,'" he suggested. "Or how about, 'She has gone home to God.' My customers love that one."

"Just 'Beloved Jenny,'" I said. "With the dates of her birth and her . . . her death."

"Not 'Our beloved daughter . . .'?"

"No." I said. "She was everyone's Jenny."

Which she was.

●

The wedding took place in a late-summer garden with Taos Mountain towering behind us. Sun and storm clouds, rain and a double rainbow, and wind blowing our hair against our lips. Still fragile as a low-fired clay jug, I invited only the people I was sure loved me. And our families. My mother arranged everything and paid for it all—the flowers, the food, the photographer. With the same loving care with which I decorated my daughter's coffin, my mother decorated me. Jeff and I made an altar with photographs of our two fathers and Jenny, calling upon them to bear witness and bless us.

My daughter had become my ancestor.

Charlene officiated the service, weaving Jenny like a thread of light throughout. We constructed a chuppah, the traditional Jewish wedding canopy, from aspen saplings. My sister held up one corner; my brother another; Jeff's sister, Linda, the third; and his brother Lance the fourth. We chanted an invocation in Sanskrit, read scriptures from the gospels of Jesus. Jeff shattered a wine glass beneath his sandaled foot, symbol of the impermanence of life and the imperative to hold it precious.

The entire ceremony was a testament to that exquisite fragility.

When I pushed Jeff's ring onto his finger, a look of astonishment crossed his face. He leaned over and whispered in my ear, "I feel like Frodo, receiving the ring of power."

"Is that a good thing or a bad thing?" I asked.

"It's a good thing," he said. "A very, very good thing. It means I am worthy."

Only then did I begin to cry.

Part 3

CHAPTER 23

Heartfulness Practice

With reticence at first, and then with mounting courage, I dared to mourn my child. From the very beginning I suspected that something holy was happening and that if I were to push it away, I would regret it for the rest of my life. There was this sense of urgency, as if turning from death meant turning from my child. I wanted to offer Jenny the gift of my commitment to accompany her on her journey away from me, even if to do so simply meant dedicating my heartbeat and my breath to her and paying attention.

And so I showed up.

When a feeling I did not think I could survive would threaten to engulf me, I practiced turning toward it with the arms of my soul outstretched, and then my heart would unclench a little and make space for the pain. Years of contemplative practice had taught me just enough to know better than to believe everything I think—how to shift from regretting the past and fearing the future to abiding with what is. In this case, a totally fucked up thing. The ultimate fucked up thing. I sat with that.

I did not engage in this practice to prove something to myself or anyone else. I was not interested in flexing my spiritual muscles. I did it for Jenny. My willingness to stay present through this process was an act of devotion. By leaning into the horror and yielding to the sorrow, by standing in the fire of emptiness and saying yes to the mystery, I was honoring my child and expressing my ongoing love for her. It was not mere mindfulness practice; it was heartfulness practice.

•

Our first Thanksgiving without Jenny was only a few weeks after her death, and Jeff and I were still in Hawaii. I was relieved to avoid a holiday dinner with my family. I didn't think I would have been able to bear the empty place at the table. I was already making plans to skip Christmas.

We went out to a restaurant on the beach and ordered fish and pretended it was any other day. But my rebellion was hollow. I couldn't maintain the façade of apathy.

"Let's write down everything we're grateful for," I abruptly suggested. You've got to be kidding me, my embittered self said to my hopeful self.

"Good idea." Jeff handed me a white paper napkin. I unfolded it and drew a line down the middle with a ballpoint pen. I wrote "J" on the left-hand column and "M" on the right, as if we were about to play a game of Rummy.

"You first," I said.

"Having had the chance to be Jenny's stepfather," he said, and I jotted that down.

"The community that's holding me," I wrote.

And our gratitude came tumbling out like rolling melons from a basket. The sunset over the South Pacific. Kirtan. My mother, and Jeff's mother, and Mother Mary. Every one of Jenny's idiosyncrasies, from the cackling sound of her laugh to the way she would wash her money and paperclip the bills on a string to dry. I wanted to collect everything about her and weave it into the fabric of my own life. I wanted to embody the best of Jenny—her fearlessness in the face of other people's opinions, her joyful exuberance, and her deep quietude--and let these things make me a better human. Her legacy would live in me.

CHAPTER 24

The Landscape of Loss

Elisabeth Kübler-Ross, pioneer of the conscious dying movement, lived to regret having described the common features of the grief journey as stages. She came to see that everyone grieves differently and that science collapses in the face of the mysteries of the heart. There is no map for the landscape of loss, no established itinerary, no cosmic checklist, where each item ticked off gets you closer to success. You cannot succeed in mourning your loved ones. You cannot fail. Nor is grief a malady, like the flu. You will not get over it. You will only come to integrate your loss, like the girl who learned to surf again after her arm was bitten off by a shark. The death of a beloved is an amputation. You find a new center of gravity, but the limb does not grow back.

When someone you love very much dies, the sky falls. And so you walk around under a fallen sky.

I became intimate with the topography of Kübler-Ross's grief world: denial, anger, bargaining, depression, acceptance. I dipped in and out of denial at first. This did not mean that I didn't get what had happened. I was brutally aware that my daughter had stopped breathing, her heart had ceased to beat, her body had grown cold and stiff and then been cut open and examined, and then it had burned and scattered and buried. But sometimes I could not take it all the way in. "Really, Jenny? Dead? What?" It was a nightmare from which I could not shake myself awake, but I could drift into a liminal space where the edges of trauma were softened a little, insulating me from shock and preventing me from going insane.

And then sometimes—especially when the loss was fresh—denial didn't feel like delusion at all, but like grace. It was as if angels came swooping into the burned-out chamber of my soul, scooping me up and rocking me in their wings. Like spring water filling a redwood trunk that had been hollowed out by a forest fire. As if the storm of loss had parted the veil that's meant to separate us from some kind of heavenly realm, and for a moment I could see it, even step through and dwell there a little. At these times—usually when my people surrounded me to chant and pray, to bring me chocolate and scented bath oils, to praise my daughter's beauty and wisdom and tell me a story of a time she made them laugh—a palpable holiness broke through the clouds of lamentation and exalted me. I could not deny the beauty. Maybe this is merely brain chemistry masquerading as mystical experience. But these two realities are not mutually exclusive. This biochemical phenomenon is in itself a divine gift. I say thank you.

Surrounded by loved ones anticipating my every wish, I spent most of those early days yearning to be left alone. I needed to focus. It took all my energy and attention to hold what had happened. Like a hedgehog protecting herself against the world, I curled in on myself and stuck out my quills. It may have looked like I was isolating, but I was only tending the broken boat of my soul. It was not pathological; it was spiritual. It was exhausting work, but it was imperative.

Then there was anger. Some people rage against God for snatching their loved ones from their lives. Others blame the dead for doing whatever self-destructive thing took them over that edge. For me, it was insufferable irritability. Everything got on my nerves, from the way my mother chewed her food to acquaintances trying to make small talk while I was pumping gas at the Chevron station. On the way home from a trip to New York I could have bitten my sister's head off for stirring the sugar into my coffee at the airport as if I could not handle such mundane matters myself and then treating me like a mental patient when I overreacted.

"I've always been this way!" I wailed in Amy's forgiving arms much later, when I had stopped shrieking and my fury had shifted into remorse. "This is how I would get with Jenny. Out of control. A goddam lunatic."

"It's grief, Honey."

"I wish I could use that excuse. But I can't. This is who I am."

I prayed Amy would not believe me.

There was a movable boundary in my psyche between anger and anxiety, and I oscillated from one to the other. In the opening line of A Grief Observed, C.S. Lewis said, "No one ever told me that grief felt so like fear." My fear lasted for years. Sometimes it was a fist of dread I carried in the pit of my stomach. Other times it was a free-floating apprehensiveness that accompanied me like a cloud of gnats around my face. Long past the age when it would have been my responsibility to monitor Jenny's whereabouts, the maternal part of me had not yet relinquished that psychic vigilance. Every time I unplugged from my regular life and went away on a trip, those primal antennae would scan for my offspring, until I became conscious of the impulse and willed myself to let go.

As hard as I tried to talk myself down, a deeper part of me was convinced that I had failed the most essential human mission: to keep my children safe at all costs, even at the cost of my own life. To find myself alive while my child was dead scrambled the program beyond repair. No matter how much healing I had done over the years, something inside would be forever damaged. Every so often, my psyche would default and try to reestablish that basic connection, and when it failed to, I became anxious and confused.

The most vexing flavor on the grief menu was bargaining. Around 2:00 in the morning I would be roused from sleep by the clanging symbols of regret: I should have, she could have, if only he would have. I would replay those final moments in the darkened street when Jenny slipped into the driver's seat and sped away in my car. I would picture her lying on the metal table in the morgue, her hands up as if shielding her body against the fatal impact. I would relive all the moments when we fought and I said stupid, mean things I could never take back. I love you, Jen, I would whisper into space and then strain to hear her say it back: I love you, Mom. But the only sound was the roaring of my own ragged breath.

I was trying to think my way through the problem of death using the wrong tool. By going around and around the same stories, my mind short-circuited, leaving me beaten and bruised. I failed again and again to resolve the predicament. Jenny remained dead.

"No, you're not going crazy," my friend Ted chuckled. "You're just grieving." Ted could get away with laughing at me. His wife, Leslie—his high school sweetheart and mother of his two daughters—had died of a brain tumor when the girls were three and five. Then both children were killed in a car crash with their grandmother, Leslie's mom, when Amy was six and Keri was nine. Ted had survived his impossible loss by dedicating himself to being of service and training as an interfaith minister. Now he led the grief support group that had become a narrow ledge on a wall of rock where I could sometimes hold on with my toes and rest for a moment.

"It's as if we had been rolling along, shooting the movie of our life, thinking we were the director of our own show and then suddenly, wham!" Ted slammed his fist into his other palm. "You get to a scene you don't like and you go, 'Cut!'" Ted held up his hands in T position. "You try to rewind and reshoot that part, but it's like the mechanism's busted. No matter how hard you try, you cannot do that part over and make it come out the way you want it." He pulled my head against his shoulder. "Sucks, doesn't it?"

I took to murmuring self-soothing proclamations whenever I began to spiral into the hell realms: "It's okay, Mirabai," or "All will be well," or "You were a good mom." I became more adept at sidestepping the freight train of bargaining when I saw it hurtling toward me. And when I did not manage to intercept the process, I learned to let it play itself out without attaching ultimate truth to my out-of-control thoughts. Eventually I would exhaust myself with masochistic scenarios, and the locomotive would slow to a halt in a cloud of noxious fumes.

That's when I would collapse into depression. But it wasn't clinical depression. It was a full-bodied sorrow that took my breath away and dropped me into profound stillness. From this quiet space I could hear the sound of my own heart at last. My vulnerable heart, my big-sky heart, my wise and beautiful heart. Unable to hold myself up any longer, I let myself down into the arms of my groundlessness, and I found refuge there. It was a relief to know nothing, to be simply sad. In the darkness, I could rest at last.

Maybe this is what Saint John of the Cross was talking about: the holy holy holy radiance of the dark night of the soul. This is what Teresa of Avila meant when she praised the beautiful wound of longing for God. "The grief you cry out from draws you toward union," Rumi said. "Your pure sadness that wants help is the secret cup." This could be that secret cup. I tipped my head. I drank.

Which is what acceptance looks like. Not like light at the end of the tunnel. Not like, now everything's going to be all right. It isn't that Jenny's death was finally okay with me and I was ready to get on with my life. It was a matter of looking loss straight in the face and not blinking. It was a taking of my own sweet self into my arms and forgiving her. What I accepted was that I could not have Jenny beside me in physical form, but my love for her—and the fire of missing her—was our connection, and she could never ever leave me.

I set about cultivating this new, metaphysical relationship with my daughter. I circled back into every phase of the grief journey a thousand times, and each time that I returned to the garden of acceptance, the trees were taller and the fruits were sweeter and new species were pushing their tender green heads up from the loam.

CHAPTER 25

Rowing Through
the Underworld

A few months after Jenny died, I spent a night at my mother's studio, trying to write some kind of chronicle of my daughter's life and death. As I was beginning to fall asleep, the candle flickering beside her picture, I had a vision: I was rowing a small boat upstream through the underworld. I could feel the dark walls towering on either side of me. I could hear the splash of my oars as they dipped into the cold water. I knew I did not belong here, but I was determined to get as far as I could before I was sent back. I wanted to follow my baby to wherever it was she had gone. She had never been this far away from me, and I had to make sure she would be okay.

Of course, she was not okay. She was dead, and there was no way I could follow her on that journey.

And she was completely okay. Nothing could ever hurt her again.

•

I have never met a bereaved mother who did not, at some point anyway—maybe in a place so secret that it was even a secret from her-self—crave death. Part of this could be attributed to suicidal despair. But there is another aspect to the desire to die after your child has died: the allure of the Other World.

You have caught a glimpse of that realm, and it has dazzled you. It is luminous and vast. It is the holiest thing you have ever seen. And your child lives there.

The mystics of all traditions bless the annihilating power of love. The highest calling of the moth is to fly into the heart of the candle flame. "I praise what is truly alive," Goethe proclaimed, "what longs to be burned to death." This is why John of the Cross considered a dark night of the soul to be very good news: it is only when night falls on the house of the ordinary faculties that the soul is able to risk slipping away for a secret rendezvous with the Beloved in the garden. This is why when Teresa of Avila had a vision of an angel plunging his flaming arrow into her womb, she never wanted it to end. This is why the hadith of the Prophet Muhammad suggests that you "die before you die." Once we have died to the false self, we have a hope of getting out of our own way and meeting the Holy One face to face.

Grief strips us. It stripped me. I couldn't help but notice that this radically naked state resembled what all my favorite mystics had been trying to teach me for decades. You can't have divine union encumbered by spiritual addictions and cosmic concepts. You can't make love with your clothes on. Now here I was, disrobed by loss, dipped in fire, pretty much annihilated. What used to make my spirit soar now left me cold, and none of my ideas about ultimate reality made any sense. What I had been trying to accomplish through years of rigorous discipline had happened overnight: a state of no self. I was ready for the holy encounter at last!

But I wasn't in the mood.

I wanted to want God. But I wanted Jenny more.

CHAPTER 26

Tia Teresa

At first I snubbed Saint Teresa of Avila. And then she saved my life.

There is no way to approach Saint John of the Cross without encountering his guru, Saint Teresa. I was attracted to John from the beginning: his quiet passion, his limpid intellect, his formality. I liked that he was a Christian who almost never felt the need to mention Christ. I loved that he loved the night sky. He reminded me of Rumi, with his preoccupation with gardens and fire and the wine of transformation. John was understated—like me—a mild exterior, barely containing a blazing heart. Like me, John found and followed the footprints of the Holy One through the emptiness.

Teresa was a drama queen. Everyone knew it, and she freely admitted it. Between her predilection for altered states of consciousness and her hunger to be liked, I found myself a bit embarrassed for her. But if my beloved John loved Teresa, there must be something worthy there. Not to mention the fact that five centuries after her last breath, people of every faith tradition and none still speak of her with awe and affection.

Which is why, after I had submitted my new translation of Dark Night of the Soul to my publisher, I agreed to translate Teresa's book, The Interior Castle. John was notoriously difficult to get. I figured Teresa might hold a key to John that I could hand to my readers. I was willing to sacrifice my personal tastes for the sake of duty.

Then my daughter died and the ground collapsed beneath me and I was hurtling through space. All plans dissolved in the magma of loss. The train of my life jumped its tracks and crashed in the desert.

The things that had felt prodigiously significant the day before Jenny's death now struck me as ridiculous. Credit card bills. Cellulite. What I was going to be when I grew up.

My editor called to express her condolences.

"We would, of course, understand completely if you needed to be released from your contract for the Teresa book," she said.

"No, thanks," I heard myself answer. "I'll do it."

What else was I going to do? I could fall backwards off the Rio Grande Gorge Bridge and tumble into the abyss, or I could try to render a sixteenth-century Spanish text accessible in English. It was a job, like stripping old key locks off hotel room doors and replacing them with electronic locks, like fixing a toilet or plowing a field. Besides, I had made the decision to observe the one-year Jewish mourning cycle, which meant gathering my attention to a single point—grieving my child—and letting go of all superfluous activities. Writing a book meant I didn't need to leave the house. Perfect.

I didn't have the energy to sweep the floor. I couldn't manage to fix a sandwich. But every day I could make my way downstairs into Jenny's old room, which Jeff had helped me convert into an office. I could prop open a copy of The Interior Castle in its original language and a couple of existing English translations for reference, an early Renaissance Spanish dictionary on my right and a complete modern version to my left, and translate what lay before me. When I had finished page seven, I would turn to page eight.

And as I turned the pages, I watched this sacred text unfold beneath my fingers like a treasure map drafted in invisible ink becoming visible when held over a candle flame. Teresa was offering a way home—not only for the readers on whose behalf I had so recently condescended to undertake this task, but also for me, newly shattered and radically disoriented.

•

Toward the end of her life, when Teresa had lived far longer than anyone (especially she) had imagined she would—given the range of illnesses, heartbreaks, and scandals she had endured—Teresa was ordered by her confessor to write a book about the insights that had unfolded since she submitted her autobiography two decades earlier. The nun and the priest had been traveling by donkey cart across the rugged landscape of northern Spain, on their way to found another new convent of Discalced (Barefoot) Carmelites, when they stopped for the night in a roadside inn. After the evening meal, they had one of those spiritual conversations old friends sometimes have that lift them off their chairs and light their hair on fire.

"But they already seized my first book," she kvetched, "and then used it against me."

The book she was referring came to be known as The Book of My Life (which I eventually got around to translating), one of the great coming-of-age stories in the canon of mystical of literature. The men who seized it were members of the Spanish Inquisition, who also happened to be the ones who ordered her to write it in the first place, insisting that she document the visions, voices, raptures, and ecstasies they kept hearing about. They then used Teresa's own account in their investigation, in an effort to determine whether these phenomena were authentic revelations or tricks of the devil. They eventually let Teresa off the hook, but they never gave the manuscript back.

Her friend the priest must have shrugged and smiled, because that night Teresa withdrew to her cell and "beseeched the Lord" to speak for her, since she "couldn't think of anything to say" and "had no idea how to begin to fulfill this particular vow of obedience."

The Lord came through with a vision of the soul as a radiant crystal palace, from the center of which the Beloved is beckoning the lover to merge with him.

"What do you think that a place might be like that such a king—so powerful and wise, so pure and filled with all good things—would find so delightful?" Teresa asks us at the beginning of The Interior Castle. "I myself can come up with nothing as magnificent as the beauty and amplitude of a soul."

As I translated these lines, I was struck by two startling implications: (1) Since the fire of missing Jenny felt uncannily similar to my lifelong yearning for God, maybe the path to an abiding connection with her was the same as the trajectory for divine union: inward. (2) Perhaps I wasn't a horrible, wretched, evil creature who had let my own child plummet to her death after all, but rather a precious jewel so exquisite that the Beloved himself would rather dwell nowhere else than inside me.

If Teresa's vision of the soul as the single place in all of creation where God would choose to hang out struck me as revolutionary, imagine how radical it must have sounded to a group of sixteenth-century nuns who had been conditioned to believe that (a) our souls are dirty and flawed, on account of original sin, and (b) any kind of relationship with the Holy One required the recitation of prescribed prayers and the intercession of a priest. But no! As it turned out, they were beautiful and perfect exactly as they were, and if they wanted to be with God, all they had to do was close their eyes and go within.

•

Profound sorrow closes old doors and opens new ones. Friends I would have expected to stay by my side as I walked through the landscape of loss peeled off and disappeared. Invisible advocates, like a Catholic nun who had lived nearly five hundred years ago, materialized.

Teresa became my companion, my solace, my refuge. Like a favorite Jewish aunt who sat me down across the table and fed me tea and ruggelah, Teresa held a sacred space for my brokenness. She patted my hand, she wept with me. She listened to me speak about my daughter—what I loved most about her, what drove me crazy, what I would give anything to do over and do right. And when I confessed that I did not really even believe in God, Teresa did not flinch. She simply chuckled and refreshed my cup of tea. "I know just what you mean, mi 'jita," she said.

CHAPTER 27

Believing Everything

I do and I do not believe in God. I believe in a life that transcends this one, and I also believe that when this life ends we cease to exist. I am not preoccupied with logical consistency. I give myself permission to believe everything, and then to stop believing that and believe something else. Any lingering hope for coming up with an ultimate answer to the problem of what happens when we die was obliterated with the death of my child.

This did not stop me from trying to determine what had become of Jenny.

I experimented with various positions:

1. She was gone. She certainly felt gone. For the first few days and weeks after the accident, her presence was still strong, but the connection grew increasingly tenuous until finally, after a month or so, I could not feel her with me anymore. This felt sense coincided with teachings from the Tibetan Book of the Dead. Forty-nine days is the turning point; the deceased has finished navigating the Bardos and moved on.

2. She was a spirit now. Like a guardian angel, like an ancestor. She guided my steps and made magical things happen, such as a flock of birds exploding from a cottonwood tree exactly as I was remembering the day we hiked to the river and tied friendship bracelets around each other's wrists to commemorate the anniversary of Jenny's adoption. I especially noticed her availability to me as my speaking career began to unfold within a couple of years of her death. Whenever I would step out onto the stage, it was as if I were making way for Jenny to step

in and speak through me. I took to invoking her outright: Okay, Jen, here we go.

3. Her soul was doing whatever it is that souls do to let go of this life and ready herself for a new one. In a couple of years, maybe, she would be reincarnated. Maybe even into our family! When some new baby was born to one of us, I would gaze into her eyes and recognize my dead daughter, and then, as the child developed, I would notice many of Jenny's mannerisms and proclivities.

4. Jenny was dwelling in some kind of beautiful afterlife. All the secrets of the universe were now revealed to her, and all the suffering of her short life—from the early childhood abuse to the explosion of brain chemistry at the end—had been redeemed. She was abiding in a love that had no beginning and would never end. Paradise.

5. She lived on only in our memories. This is what my Jewish forebears believed. And so we are meant to speak of them, and light Yartzeit candles for them, and name our offspring after them.

I ended up accepting an assortment of propositions that might seem to be mutually exclusive and yet fit easily into the broken open container of my consciousness. Jenny was no longer alive, and I couldn't pretend to know exactly what she now was instead of alive. Like a drop of water, she had returned to the sea from which we all arise. She had merged; no individuality remained. And at the same time, Jenny was an ever-living entity who was totally available to me. All I had to do was open to her, and there she would be.

•

Not long after Jenny died, my sister dreamed that we went to a restaurant, slipped into a booth, and there was Jenny, sitting beside me.

"Hi Jen-Wen!" Amy was thrilled to see her alive and well. "What are you doing here?"

"I'm always here. With my mom."

"Mirabai! Looks who's sitting next to you!" said my dream sister.

But I could not see Jenny.

"Tell her, Amy," Jenny said. "Tell her I am always with her. She just needs to turn around."

Amy tried, but my dream self could not hear her words. Or could not believe her. I shrugged and opened my dream menu. Amy glanced helplessly at her niece. Jenny smiled reassuringly.

"I'll tell her when I wake up," Amy said.

And she did.

I decided to practice tuning into my invisible child, but I couldn't hold the focus. Her absence was so much louder than her presence.

●

One night we went out to dinner with Sean and Tania to celebrate the publication of Sean's new book, One Bird, One Stone. I was still observing the ritual mourning period and did not want to be in public places if I could avoid it. Besides, I felt like the top layer of skin had been burned off and the new cells had not grown back. I was walking around raw and permeable. The world was a dangerous place.

Tania arranged for us to be seated in a closed-off section at the back of the restaurant. Pedro, the maître d', personally took care of us.

After he had opened the bottle of sparkling white wine and filled our glasses, he squatted down beside my chair and spoke to me softly, in Spanish.

"I don't know exactly how to tell you this, but your daughter just came to me with a message for you."

"Jenny?"

Pedro nodded.

"May I give it to you?"

I smiled. "Sure," I said. Pedro was not the first person to claim that my dead daughter was speaking through them. I decided to humor him. Even if—as I suspected—this was just Pedro's way of offering succor, I might as well open my heart and receive it graciously. Maybe it would help.

"The first thing is, she wants you to know that it was not your fault. Her death was her destiny. She completed the work she came to this world to do." That was just what Ram Dass had told me. "And that work was to love and to know that she was loved."

I looked away, looked back again.

"The other thing is that she was not afraid when she crashed, and she felt no pain."

Oh, how I hoped this was true!

"And, finally, Jenny wants you to know that she is always with you. All you have to do is reach out for her, and she will be right there. She is right here, right now. Do you feel her?"

I closed my eyes, setting free the tears trapped there. I shook my head. "All I feel is my broken heart," I admitted.

Pedro nodded, took my hand and held it. "In time you will be able to find her again. She is patient." Pedro rose and squeezed my shoulder. "She does not want you to suffer. She is very sorry for the pain she has caused you."

My skepticism melted, and I rested my face in my folded arms. Jeff stroked my hair. Sean and Tania sat quietly.

After I raised my head and blew my nose with the linen napkin, I managed to laugh. "Only in Taos," I said. A channeling maître d'."

"In Spanish," Sean added.

Apparently Jenny liked to make appearances in restaurants. I ordered the ravioli in her honor.

●

Ten years after Jenny's death, I contracted a rare bacterial infection in the jungles of Chiapas. By the time I flew home to Taos, I was so sick I could hardly hold up my head. I had hardly managed to keep any food in my body in ten days, and every joint blazed with pain. I had a high fever and spent the first night writhing in my bed like a fish on the deck of a boat.

In the height of my misery, it occurred to me to reach out to Jenny for help.

The moment I had this thought, I felt Jenny rushing in to enfold me, as if she had enormous cool feathers in which she cradled my fiery body. Her love was so tender and immediate I could not help but surrender to her embrace. As I lay in her arms I began to relax, and the pain subsided.

Gradually, I felt Jenny release me and begin to move away.

"No!" I wailed. "Don't leave me, Jenny!"

She came flowing right back and gathered me again in her wingspan. "I will never leave you, Mom. I am always with you."

Finally, I felt strong enough to let her go of my own volition. I thanked her for coming to me when I called, and surrendered to our separation, as I have done a thousand times.

The sound of my weeping woke Jeff, and he pulled me into his arms.

"Jenny was here," I told him. "She was just here! Can you feel her?"

What he felt was me, burning up. In the morning he took me to the emergency room.

•

I realize that the feeling we have of our loved ones being close to us immediately following their death might have more to do with us than with them. At first, propelled by shock and supported by grace, we may meet them in the field of spirit. The distancing that follows may feel like they are moving away from us, yet, as with Einstein's train analogy, that's an artifact of relativity. We're the ones who, in spite of our deep desire for connection, are slipping away, back into life.

If I had trouble coming up with a solid opinion about life after death, I was equally unsuccessful in explaining to myself why Jenny had died so young. A couple of years after Jenny died, a respected Tibetan lama came through town. He had been living in Mexico, and I was asked to interpret for his Spanish-speaking interpreter. So the lama would teach in Tibetan, his interpreter would translate the teachings into Spanish, and I would translate the translations into English. Everyone, including me, seemed to find this arrangement amusing.

As payment for my efforts, I was offered a private audience with the teacher. There was only one question on my mind: where is the meaning in the death of my daughter?

"Karma," the lama answered.

"You mean that in experiencing tragedy I have chosen an accelerated trajectory to awakening?" I asked hopefully.

"No."

"What, then, am I supposed to learn from this loss?"

"You did something terrible in a previous life," the lama said, a bit impatiently, as if it were obvious—the only possible explanation.

"You mean, this is . . . punishment?"

He nodded. The interpreter nodded. My fellow Taoseños shifted uncomfortably on their zafus.

"No hay palabra in Tibetano," the translator explained, apologetically. "Punishment, no. More like fruits ripening."

"And so Jenny's death is the ripe fruit of my previous actions."

"Si." The lama watched our interaction and smiled approvingly, as if the matter had been resolved and I could go in peace.

But I was not finished. "Couldn't it be that I chose to endure tragedy in this lifetime as a kind of steep path to enlightenment?"

The interpreter interpreted, and the lama, once again, shook his head.

"Or maybe that I took on this suffering on behalf of all sentient beings?"

"No, not possible."

"I deserve this loss."

Apparently so. The lama was finished with our interview. He gathered his robes and rose, followed by his interpreter and a small entourage.

I tried this on, but I had grown too accustomed to my spiritual nudity and so I removed it and went back to bare unknowingness.

●

I think Jenny understood more about all this than I did. Death, deathlessness. I think the traumas of her early childhood yanked the gate between the worlds right off its hinges, and she gained VIP access to realms the rest of us are barred from. I knew from the moment I met her that this little being was wise far beyond her four years.

By the time she was six, my miniature daughter had doubled in weight, shot up half a foot, and her vocabulary leapt from around a dozen pretty much unintelligible words to a flowing commentary on every amazing ordinary detail of the world around her. She had also forgotten everything that happened to her before she came to live with me.

Except for a couple of incidents, which occupied a hazy corner of her memory until the day she died.

In one memory, Jenny is a princess. She is living at All Faiths Receiving Home in Albuquerque, and someone lifts her onto a throne. They set a jeweled tiara on her head and place a gilded wand in her hand. They curtsy and bow. They sing "Happy Birthday." She is fed the creamiest delicacies, and she can stay up as late as she pleases. She is surprised by her royal status, but she accepts her situation calmly, with a mixture of glee and resignation.

In the other memory, Jenny is riding her Big Wheel through the trailer park where she lives with her Aunt Pauline, who is "sick" and cannot take care of her. She rumbles along the broken sidewalk and comes upon a man lying in the dried up grass. His eyes are closed. As she looks at him, she sees a second body rise out of his regular body. It sits up, looks around, glances down at the one lying beneath it, and then floats into the sky and out of sight.

•

One of the methods I use to torture myself is to replay all the ways in which I failed to make Jenny's childhood perfect. Instead of remembering the scavenger hunts in which I composed rhyming poems for every clue, or climbing the pyramids of Monte Albán and Chichen Itza together, or making a handmade card every year on Jenny's birthday with a different version of "You are the light of my life" encircled by a heart with rays bursting out of it, I dwell on the days when I was selfish and boring.

Like this one:

I'm braiding her hair and tucking her in, leaning to kiss her forehead.

"Mom, can we do the Cloud?"

"Not tonight, Jen, I'm tired."

"You're always tired."

I sigh. She's right. Tonight (like Mama Sisyphus) I will roll my rock up the hill.

I begin. "You are standing at the bottom of a staircase. Climb up. Slowly. Step by step, breath by breath, until you reach the top. You are in front of a beautiful door. You turn the knob, and it opens. You step out onto a platform in the middle of the sky."

Her eyes are closed. I can see the movement of her smile muscles in the dim room.

"You look around. The sky is clear and blue. A perfect puffy white cloud in the distance. The cloud is drifting toward you. Closer and closer. Now it is hovering in front of you. Jump onto the cloud."

In her imagination, my daughter throws herself onto the pillow of sky.

"Your cloud begins to drift away. You are safe, cradled in its softness. You turn over and look down. You can see the land below you. Rolling hills, sparkling rivers, meadows filled with wildflowers. In the distance is the ocean, waves crashing on the shore. Two unicorns are cantering along the beach, their horns flashing gold in the sunlight. They look up at you and smile."

I can see her now, leaning over her pillowy chariot, blowing kisses to the magical beings below. We sit in silence for a while as Jenny tracks the unicorns along the shore.

"Now it is time to go back home, back to your own bed. Your cloud carries you to the platform in the sky. You step off, and you are standing in front of the door. You open it and walk slowly down the staircase, step by step, breath by breath. And now you are lying in your bed, ready for sleep. Good night, my angel."

She snuggles into the covers and grows still.

After Jenny died, I remembered all the nights I didn't do the Cloud, all the times I succumbed to my fatigue, my desire to be done with the day, until gradually she stopped asking, and the Cloud evaporated. I rationalized that Jenny was too old for the Cloud. But no one is ever too old to be taken on a journey through the sky. How could I have let the magic go?

After Matty died, Mom could not listen to Pete Seeger sing "Puff the Magic Dragon" without crying. It was this line that undid her: "Dragons live forever, but not so little boys." My mother would have done anything to keep the magic alive. And I tossed it away like a like a pair of shoes that had grown too small.

Shoes made of magic never grow too small.

CHAPTER 28

Dog Medicine

Jenny sent a team of dog angels to my rescue after she was gone. They did not always act angelically. Hobbes died. Ziggy bit people and then died. Isaiah shot across the horizon of our hearts like a nova for five years, and then he disappeared. Dying angels are not exactly my prescription for healing, but they each seemed to fulfill their appointed task—prior to and because of their untimely deaths.

When I first got together with Jeff, he made it clear that he was not interested in adding a dog to the family, and the subject did not arise again. But after Jenny died, I did not know what to do with all the nurturing energy I had been accustomed to pouring onto my child. My heart was a teacup, and my love was hot tea filling up and spilling over, scorching my hand and soaking my clothes. Drenched and burning, I turned my thoughts to a puppy.

And so Jeff agreed to a scouting trip to the animal shelter, and we came home with a four-month-old German shepherd–Australian shepherd mix whom we named Hobbes, in honor of Jenny's favorite philosopher—not Thomas Hobbes, the stuffy British social theorist, but Calvin's imaginary sidekick. Hobbes punctuated my bouts of leaden despair with moments of unalloyed joy. He was devoted from the beginning and seemed to know exactly how to tend my heart. The one and only day he found his way off our property, he was killed by a car a few yards away from our house and bled to death beneath a statue of Saint Francis that Father Bill had placed in his front yard next door. concluded that Saint Francis had sent Hobbes to get me through the most arduous leg of my grief journey, and that when his work was done, he had moved on to minister to some other brokenhearted mother. But I wouldn't survive another loss. No more dogs.

A few months later, however, I found myself driving to the animal shelter in a trance and returning with the most ridiculous looking little creature I had ever seen—a mix of about a dozen radically different breeds, but predominantly blue heeler and Chihuahua. He had black and white speckles, a pink belly, and an exaggerated underbite. We named him Ziggy. Our newest family member alternated between dissolving into blissful sleep in our arms and periodically snapping at our faces with no provocation. Ziggy, too, managed to slip out of the yard and collide with a car driving far too fast on our rural road. We buried him next to Hobbes.

My yearning for another dog was proportionate to my missing Jenny. I sat with that. I let it burn. And then one day the phone rang.

"Hi, Honey, it's your friend Elaine," said my friend Elaine. "What are you doing?"

"Reading," I lied. I was sleeping. A bereaved father named Alan told me that when his son was killed in a car accident his boss had asked him if he was having trouble sleeping, and Alan had answered that no, it was being awake he was having trouble with. Me too.

"Can you meet me at Cid's?" Cid's was our local natural foods store, a place I had been avoiding, since I knew at least fifty percent of the people who shopped there, and everybody seemed to have a different story they told themselves about my loss. "There is an adorable basket of puppies in the parking lot. The guy says he's going to drown whichever ones are left at the end of the day."

"That is so not fair, Elaine. How can I possibly say no?"

"You can't. Look, I'll get one and you get one. That way when you travel I can take care of your puppy, and when I go away you can take care of mine. Our dogs will be sisters!" That was a good idea, actually. "There's this tiny one with pale green eyes and freckles. She looks like you."

"Oh, great."

"How soon can you be here? I'll wait."

Never, I should have said. I can't love another being. I have nothing left. Besides, I promised Jeff. Our dog days were over.

"Twenty minutes."

"Great, I'll be the lady with a puppy in each arm."

And so it was that Gita came into my life. Gita, my special needs dog, who had one thing and another wrong with her from the moment she crept in the door and rushed to hide under the bed—a broken tail, inexplicable fevers, skin irritations. She was afraid of everything, and I developed a palette of behaviors to accommodate her anxieties. Yet once I had earned Gita's trust, she venerated me with singular devotion, and she read my thoughts so effortlessly that any training was redundant. Elaine's dog Ramona succumbed to one of the same mysterious illnesses that struck Gita, but Gita lived on.

After Ramona's death, Gita was depressed. Her coat grew dull, and she was no longer interested in taking walks.

"She needs a companion," I said.

"Oy vey," said Jeff, but it was difficult to disagree.

It was embarrassing to go to the shelter for the third time, with two dead dogs on our record. But this time we had a foolproof containment system. We installed an expensive "invisible fence" with shock collars. Our new puppy, whom we named Isaiah after the prophet of peace, had the system beat within a week. But he lasted five years. Isaiah was by far the most beautiful of all my dog angels. He had long golden red fur and eyes like chocolate stars. He was enthusiastic, tender, and hopelessly untrainable. Isaiah adored Gita, and she made a show of putting up with his affections. But after Isaiah disappeared one cold December night when Jeff and I were out to dinner for Amy's birthday, Gita mourned him as fiercely as I did.

It took us a year to say yes to another dog. On the day that Jenny would have turned twenty-five, we adopted Lola, an accidental mix of two show dogs: a keeshond and a German pinscher. Lola bounded into the house, plopped down on Jeff's feet, and gazed up into his face. Then, as if shot out of a cannon, she bounced from one corner of the house to another before collapsing on the floor and falling asleep. Terrified, smitten, we welcomed Lola into the family, where she has been entertaining us with her cleverness, driving us crazy with her hyperactivity, and melting our hearts with her kindness ever since.

And now Gita is growing old, little by little letting go of this life, sinking into a slow pool of quietude, and I feel ready. Hers is a rightful passage, developmentally appropriate. I will miss her, and I bless her on her way.

CHAPTER 29

Rarified

You know how the air becomes rarified when the storm of loss blows through? Charged with light. A gleaming border surrounding every leaf and eyelash. An electrical current bathing your spine as you shop for peaches and unclip the laundry from the line. As if you had been turned inside out by the darkness, rendered exquisitely singular. Almost chosen, like a prophet or a princess. And how the rest of the world goes on in its inane everydayness, oblivious to the sanctity of the broken-open sky in which you now abide?

The first time I remember this feeling is after Matty had died over Christmas vacation, and when I got back to school, I was different from every other third-grader. There was no treatment for my condition, and no one even asked what my symptoms were. The next time was when Mom left Dad and ran away to Mexico with Ramón and then called for me to meet them at the border. As I climbed on that bus headed for El Paso, the sun was setting on Taos. I took my seat and looked out the window as my town went about its regular business, and I couldn't believe they did not realize how momentous it was that my parents were splitting up for good and I was hurtling alone through space.

But the deepest chasm of all cracked open when Jenny died. The casual manner with which grocery checkers rang up my purchases and bank tellers cashed my checks accentuated my alienation. In light of my loss, their bored expressions struck me as sacrilegious, even though I rationalized that they had no way of knowing what had happened. And if they were rude to me, I wanted to have them arrested. When

I described this feeling to my old friend and mentor, Asha, on the phone, she said she had always fantasized launching a black armband campaign for the bereaved. Then whenever some officious bureaucrat or apathetic stranger treated us with anything less than reverence, we could simply flash our encircled biceps, and they would bow. A grieving mom named Kirry, whose two-month-old baby had died, told me she felt like a red carpet should unfurl every time her car pulled up and she stepped onto the curb.

As Jeff was kneeling on that dock that day at Hanalei Bay and a southerly swell crashed against the pilings and lifted Jenny's ashes from his hands, a couple of young guys were leaning over the railing around fifty feet behind us, pointing to the shore break and calculating surfing conditions.

"What a world," Jeff said later. "Two people who lost their daughter scattering her ashes in the sea, and two surfers talking about waves." Grateful that, for a moment, I was not alone in my status as an alien, I smiled. "I wonder if they had any idea," he mused. "But why would they? Why should they?"

They should because a child had died, and we were her parents, and the sky should open for people like us and light our path forevermore.

●

It's easy to speculate about who Jenny would have turned into if she had lived. Our family used to do that with Matty. Every few years we would wonder aloud what he would be doing now: at eighteen, at thirty, at fifty-five. Maybe he would be an activist, volunteering in Africa or New York City. Or living on an island, building boats and raising babies. By the time Jenny was nine years old she had her sights set on Harvard Medical School. Would she be on her way to manifesting that dream now? How about now?

Or would she be living on the streets somewhere, dancing with the goddess in the temple inside her head, growling at anyone she perceived as a threat? Would the mania that took her over the mountain to her death have killed her in some other way? If Jenny had survived the onset of bipolar disorder, she would have lived with mental illness—either managing it with drugs that muffled her holy genius or forgoing intervention and spiraling into a vortex of mad joy and paralyzing despair. Either way, my-daughter-the-doctor is a fantasy. And so is my-big-brother-the-activist-artist. Matty had a brain tumor that invaded his little body and killed him. Jenny went crazy and died.

But I have trouble holding onto the facts. After Jenny's accident, our family therapist said, "Please understand, Mirabai: if Jenny had lived she would have been a torment to herself and to you for the rest of your life." I translated that statement like this: "Mirabai, it is a blessing that Jenny died in that accident, because if she had not, your life would be a living hell forevermore." I don't know if I would have tolerated such a pronouncement from anyone else. But I trusted Larry, and something in me understood that he was right.

Still, certain milestones would devastate me. When Jenny's high school class graduated, the seniors walked down the aisle carrying a framed picture of their dead friend, and they placed it on a chair beside them on stage. The headmaster—one of my oldest friends, who had drifted out of my life years before—handed out diplomas to the living graduates and then called me up to give me an honorary certificate for Jenny. We wept in each other's arms while the entire gathering made a space for this sad thing on their happy day. I hung the document in my office for a while (Jenny's old bedroom), until the fantasy began to unravel and I took it down and put it away. Later, as Jenny's friends began coupling up and reproducing, my heart would contract with sorrow with each new wedding and birth, even as I blessed the particular flowering of their aliveness.

Whenever I would witness parents yelling at their children at the aquarium or showing more interest in texting on their smart phones than watching their smart children navigate the monkey bars at the park, I would stifle the impulse to charge forth and shake them: Don't you know how fucking precious this is? Wake up! Still, to this day, when I see a mother and a teenage daughter jogging together or shopping for jeans, my envy takes my breath away. I would give anything to listen to the music my daughter had downloaded onto her device or feel her rest her head on my shoulder in an airplane.

And the truth is, I would endure losing her again and again to institutions and homelessness and the wasteland of psycho-pharmaceuticals if it meant I could hold her in my arms one more time and tell her that I love her. That I love her forever, no matter what. Doctor or prostitute. Nobel Laureate or broken blue goddess.

CHAPTER 30

The Secret Medicine

"There is a secret medicine given only to those who hurt so hard they cannot hope," Rumi promises. "The hopers would feel slighted if they knew."

When Jenny died, all my spiritual practices failed me. I could not meditate, and the very thought of silent sitting infuriated me, as if someone were offering a Band-Aid to slap over a gunshot wound. Rituals were for regular people—people who were busy navigating the mundane obstacles of everyday life—not for those who have been stripped, shattered, and blessed by tragedy. Reading had always been my refuge. Now the only thing I could bear to read was literary fiction; I craved beauty, not philosophy. Sacred scriptures were written in a code I could not decipher, and I lacked the energy to try. Self-help books sounded ridiculous, presumptuous, and whenever I picked one up I would have the urge to throw it across the room. None of the tricks I had developed over decades on the spiritual path were adequate for mending my brokenness.

Meanwhile, my career as a translator of the Christian mystics began to flower. Book after book unfolded, each one reflecting some facet of Christian wisdom teachings. Various publishers invited me to write something for their particular house, and the invitations were seductive. I accepted them all, and then I had trouble keeping them sorted out. My publishing promiscuity could have gotten me in trouble except that I was upfront about my non-monogamous proclivities. Speaking and teaching invitations started flowing in, and I found myself in the position of being the contemporary translator of the Spanish mystics in particular and a leading voice in Christian mysticism in general.

This was fine, except I was not a Christian. I was a Jewish agnostic with Pagan inclinations, a lifelong devotion to a Hindu guru (Neem Karoli Baba), an established Buddhist meditation practice (currently on hold), and an abiding connection with at least three Sufi orders. The one religion missing from my interspiritual youth was Christianity. As Jews, my family had recoiled from Jesus language. Now I caught myself apologizing to my Jewish relatives, minimizing my work among my Eastern-leaning friends, and overexplaining to strangers on airplanes what it is I do for a living.

The more successful I became in my field, the more bewildered I grew. How had this happened? I was a wild bird trapped in a gilded cage. Every day I received tasty morsels, fresh water, clean straw. But no one understood me when I cried out, "You've got the wrong bird!" They thought I was singing.

And yet with each book I wrote, my heart healed a little. Every one of the masterpieces of mystical literature I translated offered me a dose of secret medicine. But my preconceived notions of Christianity, coupled with a severe case of dark night of the soul, obscured my ability to recognize what was happening.

John of the Cross was teaching me to rest in radical unknowingness. Teresa of Avila was rekindling my yearning for union with the Beloved. Francis of Assisi was inspiring me to renew my vow to minister to those on the margins. Hildegard of Bingen was showing me how to praise God's greening energy rippling throughout the natural world. Our Lady of Guadalupe was reconciling indigenous wisdom and Christian theology in my own troubled heart. The Archangel Michael was infusing me with the fearlessness of the spiritual warrior.

Everything I needed to make my way through the landscape of loss—navigating by starlight, subsisting on nettles and honey—was hidden inside the body of work I was busy trying to escape. "One day I will graduate from these Christians," I consoled myself. "I will speak in my own voice."

Which is what I am doing now.

And which (I see at last) I could not possibly have done without the Christian wisdom figures who lit my path and kept me safe and cradled my broken heart with boundless generosity and tenderness.

It is through his friends—both living and long dead—that I have come to know and love Christ. Lucky for me, the Prince of Peace has never demanded that I swear sole allegiance to him. He seems to venerate my interspiritual heart and bless my bridge-building hands. This makes me love him all the more.

•

Dear Daddy, Matty, Phillip, and Jenny,

I've stopped hating October—the last month I remember playing with my big brother before he was taken one last time to the.hospital. The last month I touched my daughter's face before she drove my chariot into the sky and never returned. Now I watch the aspens turning colors on Taos Mountain outside my office window. "Writing is eighty percent not writing," I reassure my little brother (who, in his mid-forties, is composing his own version of our counter-culture childhood. It's very, very good, you'd be pleased to know). Now the nameless sorrow that used to seep into my heart this time of year has a name.

Ours is not a caravan of despair.

Randy Sanders died last spring, on the first day of my writing retreat in Costa Rica, where I had gone to finish telling the story of Jenny's death. He was in a nursing home by then, suffering from severe dementia. I had not seen him in many years and had no inclination to do so. "He's already taken enough from you," Mom pointed out, very practically, when Randy Sanders's first wife wrote to suggest that I visit him in the facility. I agreed. This decision helped snap the last cords that bound me to him: the threads of resentment. It's not exactly like I forgave him; it's just that what happened didn't really matter anymore. Bewilderingly, his death reopened the door of communication between his kids and me. This has been an alive and loving thing. I'm a little sacred about what they'll think of this memoir, but I have to tell my truth. All four of you taught me that.

Thanks a lot for bequeathing me the soul of a poet, Dad. (I'm only half-sarcastic, here.) I still can't help but wonder why acute sensitivity to the beauty of this world seems to come with an equal measure of permeability to pain, but I've come to accept this package. When you told me that your urge to drink was a misplaced desire for transcendence, I believed you. I believe you still. There have been a hundred times since your death when I have had the spontaneous thought, Oh, Dad would love this recipe, or, My father would be proud of my writing career, and these moments are accompanied by a sweet ache I cherish. You weren't so skilled at parenting, but you were an interesting human being, and I know you loved me.

Matty, the other night Amy and I were looking through boxes of old photographs to put in an album we're making for Mom's eightieth birthday. We found pictures of you we had not seen in years—images of the full spectrum of your ten years of life—and we came to know you all over again. Our invisible brother, who hovered over our complicated childhood like an angel with a limitless wingspan. Whose death left us with a fierce devotion to each other. As if your love were the glue pressing the other siblings together. You enfold us still.

In a small valise where Grandpa Jack kept his mementos, I found a letter I had written to him, telling him how sad I was that Grandpa Minnie had "gone to her heavenly rest" (where in the world did a seven-year-old Jewish child come up with that?) and reminding him that my brother, his grandson, was now in the hospital. "When they put the stone up where Grandma is buried, could they put this note on it?" I wrote. I drew two lines, one with a yes under it, and the other with a no, and instructed him to mark his answer on the appropriate line. "Yes, my darling," Grandpa wrote. But he kept Grandma's note, in which I inform her that I cry every night for her and also for my sick brother. The tenderness of my little-girl heart brings me to my knees now.

It was the fuel of your death, Phillip, that blasted me like a rocket across the universe and into the arms of God.

When I wrote your eulogy, Jenny, only days after your sudden death, I recklessly vowed to write your story. It has taken me thirteen years to fulfill my promise, but I offer it to you now. This is my love song to you, my baby. A lullaby to lull you to sleep. Sweet dreams, pedazo de mi corazon.

Epilogue

Nine years after Jenny's death, I stood on the bridge over the Little Ganga at Kainchi, Maharaj- -ji's ashram in the foothills of the Himalayas. It was dawn. I had been up since four, enacting the timeless traditions of India: wake to the sound of gongs and bells; bathe with a bucket; gather prayer book, prayer beads, prayer shawl; and head to the temple for morning meditation. Move from deity to deity—Lakshmi, Shiva, Hanuman—offering songs like flowers at their feet.

I had been preparing for this pilgrimage all my life.

When Jenny was around eight years old, we began saving for a trip to India. I set up a gallon pickle jar next to the woodstove and dropped loose change into the slot whenever it occurred to me. But it was too easy to rob our modified piggy bank when finances were tight, intending to replenish the amount—with interest—as soon as I was solvent. Which never happened. Then Jenny started high school, and I promised that we would go to Kainchi as a graduation present. I would have four years to get the money together.

Jenny died in her freshman year.

Nine, according to the late American sage Ian Starr, is the number of completion in many esoteric traditions. Nine days of Navaratri leading to Durga Puja. Nine Durga Pujas since the full-moon night of Jenny's death. And now here I was, honoring the ninth anniversary of Jenny's transformation in the place where it all began: the little temple in the mountains near the border of Nepal where decades ago Ram Dass sat with Maharaj-ji, and the ripple from that encounter transfigured a hundred thousand lives. Mine. Jenny's.

I had come here to complete something.

I leaned over the railing. The full moon was setting in the west, and the first rays of sunrise were tumbling over the walls of the canyon, dropping into the stream, and bouncing off the boulders. I took a tiny packet of human ashes from my satchel and opened it into the air. They drifted to the water below. These were not Jenny's ashes I was releasing, but rather a small pinch of the burnt body of the son of a woman I did not know, who had asked me to carry this trace of him to the sacred land where our mutual guru had lived. Someone had done this service for me once, and it seemed right to pass the blessing on to another bereaved mother.

The sun climbed with more confidence into the morning sky, and I moved from the upstream side of the bridge to the downstream side, to accompany the flow of ashes with my eyes. I called on Jenny to befriend this man-child and help him navigate his journey beyond the body, and on Maharaj-ji to protect him in his blanket of love. Suddenly a pair of monkeys came scrambling down the banks of the river and splashed into the water. They began to play. They lifted handfuls of river water and poured them over each other's heads, shrieking with joy. They chased each other, ran away, leapt into each other's arms and ricocheted off. Then they both paused, looked up at me on the bridge, and for a moment became as still as stone, before promptly resuming their monkeyshines.

I let magical thinking have its way with me and recognized our dead children greeting each other in these joyous monkey bodies, cavorting in the ancient land of the yogis, blessed by the king of monkeys, the incarnation of Hanuman himself, Neem Karoli Baba. Why not?

The monkeys disappeared into the forest, and I headed back through the temple gates for chai. As I was crossing the courtyard, a rustle of excitement passed through the devotees gathered there. Sri Siddhi-Ma, Baba's successor, was emerging from her rooms. Everyone rushed into position to prostrate themselves at her feet. I drifted toward the front of the crowd. Ma walked over to where I was standing, and our eyes met. She did not smile, yet her gaze exuded a kind of childlike mischief and delight.

"Ah, Mira," she said.

"Pranam," someone behind me whispered. I dropped to my knees and pressed my whole torso against the stone floor at Mata-ji's feet. I rested my right hand on her socks.

Philosophically, I did not really approve of the practice of bowing to another human being. "The age of the guru is over," I had preached. "This is a time of collective awakening, of mutual empowerment. We are the ones we have been waiting for." Etcetera, etcetera. But the urge to pranam before this elderly being, who was revered as a saint, overrode my opinion on the matter. Oh, just this once, I thought. Just to see what it's like.

Here's what it was like: It was like becoming snowmelt and flowing down a mountainside into a waiting lake. It was like meeting ten thousand years of Vedic history in my own body. It was like finding a cave in the snow where a fire is burning and a kettle of stew is simmering. It was ordinary and holy and utterly appropriate.

When I rose, Mata-ji was speaking to her attendant in Hindi, who turned and said to me in English, "Mother will see you this afternoon."

I floated through the day in a state of radical simplicity. Being at Kainchi untied my knots. I did not worry about anything. Everything pleased me.

"Your daughter was a great being," Mata-ji said to me later, as I sat at her feet in her private room at the back of the ashram. "She died at exactly the right time, in the perfect place."

My eyes filled with tears.

"Don't cry." She shook her head and wagged her finger. "She is with you. She guides your steps."

I wiped my eyes.

"Now," said Mata-ji, "what special thing happened this morning?"

I was about to tell her about the ashes and the monkeys when I remembered. "The amrit," I said. "It was delicious." Mata-ji pressed her hands together and beamed at me.

Today was the celebration of Rasa Lila.

In the Hindu tradition, the first full moon of autumn commemorates the mythic night when Krishna, Lord of Love, danced with the gopis (milkmaids) in the moonlight, fulfilling the deepest desire each maiden hid in her heart. The day before, devotees prepare khir, a sweet rice pudding, and leave it outside all through the night where it soaks in the juices of the moon and is transformed into amrit: divine ambrosia.

Siddhi Ma herself cooks pots of khir in the ashram kitchen and sets them on the roof under the full moon, and then serves the sacred mixture to temple guests for breakfast the next day.

In this moment, I felt that Mata-ji saw into my girlhood heart—the longing, the betrayal, the cynicism, and the poetry. My darshan was probably complete. A dozen other devotees—Indians and Westerners—were waiting for their chance to sit at the feet of the Mother and ask for guidance.

"Any other questions?" Mata-ji said.

"Did she suffer when she died?"

There. That was the question that had been smoldering in the pit of my belly for nine years. But how could this old woman, who lived in a place that had been forgotten by time, possibly have an answer to the complicated set of conditions that took my daughter's life, let alone address Jenny's subjective state?

"She died in joy," Mata-ji said.

I bowed my head. I touched her feet. She raised my chin, looked into my eyes, and said it again.

"She died in joy."

Acknowledgments

How mysterious it is to me that certain people who have been so significant on my journey and who I love so much did not make their way into this book—or maybe only in passing. The story took on a life of its own, and I tried to surrender and trust that it was unfolding as it must.

And so I take the opportunity here to offer my deepest bow to those who have held my broken heart, in one way or another, as I navigated a path of grieving and transforming—an adventure that continues.

Bill McNichols, Jenny Bird, Jessie Martin, Elaine Sutton, Asha Greer, Anthony Mercolino, Charlene McDermott, Johnno Ryan, Satrupa Kagel, John Kane, Adair Ferdon, Dan Kuehn, Kim Kirschenfeld, Martha Ingalls, Tessa Bielecki, David Denny, Natalie Goldberg, Rameshwar Das, Ram Dass, Stephen and Ondrea Levine, Trudy Goodman, Sharon Salzberg, Pema Chodren, Sean Murphy, Tania Casselle, Nancy Laupheimer, Vishu Magee, Karen Pettit, Annapurna Sydell, Azima Melita Kolin, Joanne Cacciatore, Larry Schreiber, Larry Sargent, Ted Wiard, Janet Schreiber, Kelly Notaras, Haven Iverson, Marilyn Pranno, Marie Rubie, Tot Tatarsky, Clive Bridges, and the Kenney family.

Profound gratitude to my agent and friend, Sarah Jane Freymann, who has carried my story like a treasure since we first met, not long after Jenny's death, and made sure that it was shared at last. Thank you, Tami Simon, for recognizing the power of the human condition and encouraging me to tell my version of it. I am grateful that Amy Rost was my editor, because she is wise and precise and affirming and lovely.

To my family, my endless and bottomless thanks: Jenny's grandma, Susanna, and her companion, John; Jenny's grandpa, Ramón; Jenny's aunt, Amy; Jenny's uncle, Roy; Jenny's sisters, Daniela and Kali;

Jenny's cousins, Nick and Ian; Jenny's niece and nephews, Jacob, Bree, and Niko; Jenny's stepsisters, Ganga and Yamuna, and their children, Metztli, Sol, and Naya. And may the memory of my father, Ian, and my brother, Matty, be a blessing always.

Finally, with overflowing gratefulness, I acknowledge Jenny's stepfather, Ganga Das Jeff Little, who married me in the midst of my deepest sorrow, and whose love leads me home.

About the Author

Mirabai Starr writes creative nonfiction and contemporary translations of sacred literature. She is an adjunct professor of philosophy and
world religions at the University of New Mexico-Taos and teaches and
speaks internationally on contemplative practice and interspiritual
dialog. A certified bereavement counselor, Mirabai helps mourners
harness the transformational power of loss. She has received critical
acclaim for her revolutionary new translations of Dark Night of the
Soul by sixteenth-century Spanish mystic St. John of the Cross, The
Interior Castle and The Book of My Life, by St. Teresa of Avila, and
The Showings of Julian of Norwich. She is author of the six-volume
Sounds True series Contemplations, Prayers, and Living Wisdom. Her
poetry collection, Mother of God Similar to Fire, is a collaboration
with iconographer William Hart McNichols. God of Love: A Guide
to the Heart of Judaism, Christianity and Islam—winner of the New
Mexico/Arizona Book Award for Religion and the Nautilus Gold
Award in Western Spirituality, and named one of the Best Spiritual
Books of 2012 by Spirituality & Practice—positions Mirabai at the
forefront of the emerging interspiritual movement. She lives with her
extended family in the mountains of northern New Mexico.

About Sounds True

Sounds True is a multimedia publisher whose mission is to inspire and support personal transformation and spiritual awakening. Founded in 1985 and located in Boulder, Colorado, we work with many of the leading spiritual teachers, thinkers, healers, and visionary artists of our time. We strive with every title to preserve the essential "living wisdom" of the author or artist. It is our goal to create products that not only provide information to a reader or listener, but that also embody the quality of a wisdom transmission.

For those seeking genuine transformation, Sounds True is your trusted partner. At SoundsTrue.com you will find a wealth of free resources to support your journey, including exclusive weekly audio interviews, free downloads, interactive learning tools, and other special savings on all our titles.

To learn more, please visit SoundsTrue.com/freegifts or call us toll-free at 800-333-9185.